BEYOND JESUS

BEYOND JESUS

Reflections on the Gospels for the B-Cycle

Joseph G. Donders

ORBIS BOOKS
Maryknoll, New York

DOVE COMMUNICATIONS
Melbourne, Australia

The Catholic Foreign Mission Society of America (Maryknoll) recruits and trains people for overseas missionary service. Through Orbis Books Maryknoll aims to foster the international dialogue that is essential to mission. The books published, however, reflect the opinions of their authors and are not meant to represent the official position of the society.

Library of Congress Cataloging in Publication Data

Donders, Joseph G.
  Beyond Jesus.

  Includes index.
  1. Bible. N.T. Gospels—Meditations. I. Title.
BS2555.4.D65   1984   242'.3   84-5088
ISBN 0-88344-049-0 (pbk.)

Published in Australia in 1984 by Dove Communications, Box 316 Blackburn, Victoria 3130

Dove ISBN 0-85924-299-4

CONTENTS

INTRODUCTION

His disciples had been with him
for quite some time.
We don't know exactly for how long.
Some say one year,
others say two years,
and there are even some others who speak
of three years.
It is obvious from all the reports
that reached us
that he was the center of their common lives,
and also the center of their personal lives.
They had seen him
working his miracles;
they had seen him
healing the sick;
they had seen him
changing the world
around them,
and in the process
they themselves had been changing
too.
Their relationships
had been very stimulating,
very enriching,
and very pleasant.
But at the same time
those relationships
had had something rather childish,
something immature.

In his presence
they felt
that things could be left
to him;
that questions should be answered
by him;
that all change should come
from him.

>In his presence
>they felt
>like waiting for him
>in all and everything;
>they felt in a way
>no further need
>at all.

They followed,
they listened,
they imitated,
they mimicked
all he did,
all he said,
all he decided.

>They were like later
>that brother of Francis of Assisi
>would be,
>imitating Francis
>in all and everything.

That brother reasoned:
"Francis is a saint.
I want to be a saint.
If I do what Francis does
I will be like him,
I will be a saint!"

>And he started to do
>what Francis did
>all the time.
>When Francis went on his knees,
>he went on his knees;
>when Francis bowed his head,
>he bowed his head;

when Francis took two bites of bread,
he took two bites of bread.
Until Francis
got fed up with him.
They had been a bit
like that.
No wonder,
that they remained staring
after him,
when he finally left
and disappeared,
getting smaller and smaller,
behind a large, lit-up
cloud.

Before he left,
he had told them:
"I am telling you the truth,
it is better for you
that I go away,
because if I do not go,
the helper will not come
to you!"
If I do not go away
you will remain staring at me,
being nobodies yourselves.
If I do not go away
you will never realize who you are,
you will not find in yourselves
your content
and your spirit.
If I do not go away
you will never look
beyond me,
beyond Jesus,
doing your work,
living your lives
in view of
God's kingdom
on earth
and all time to come.

It is in that sense
that we at Saint Paul's,
students and staff of the University of Nairobi,
in the company of hundreds and hundreds of guests,
from all over the world,
reflected on ourselves
and on our task
in this world.
There is nowadays again
that old tendency
to reduce Jesus Christ
to the center of our lives
in a way
that makes some blind and deaf,
mute and paralyzed
in the world
in which we live.
We tried to break through
that passivity and immobility,
not thinking *only* about
personal happiness,
peace of mind,
and being saved,
but looking
beyond all this,
faithful to his word and work,
his feelings and inspiration,
drawing the consequences of his departure,
believing that he will come back,
and knowing
that while we are reaching
out to him,
in our struggle to establish
his kingdom on earth,
he is reaching out
to us.
He, our saviour
and unforgettable brother
Jesus Christ.

1.

NOT ONLY IN THE END

Mark 13: 33–37

There was never a time
in history
that humanity was looking more forward
to a change,
to a new start,
than it is now.
        The international armaments race
        in which almost all the blood and sweat
        of human work
        is spent on undoing humanity;
        the national increase of corruption,
        of scandals,
        and of the greed
        that makes each think of self
        only;
        the collapse of so many families
        and our unsatisfactory
        interpersonal human relations;
            we all cry
            with the prophet Isaiah:
            "O Lord, return!
            Our sins blew us away!

      Lord, you are our father,
      we the clay,
      you the potter,
      we are the work of your hand!''
It is amid all that hope,
amid that expectation,
that we should situate
the very simple gospel-story
of the man
who goes out
and who tells his watchman
to keep awake.
That man must have been living in a world
so uncertain
and so insecure
that he had all the bolts and the locks
at the inside of his gate,
so that you could only open it
from within his compound.
      He tells his watchman
      to stay awake.
      He does not tell him
      when he is coming back.
      He wanted to prevent the man
      from leaving his post.
      He told him:
      I might come back
      any time:
            in the evening,
            at midnight,
            at cockcrow,
            at dawn,
            so stay awake!
            And he went.
We are compared to that watchman,
to that doorkeeper,
to that custodian,
and we are advised
to stay awake

so that when the Lord comes
we are ready.
And, of course,
we should be!
> But the story is about more
> than just that!
> It is a gospel
> that determines
> a whole dimension in our lives.
> It is a gospel
> about something that keeps us busy
> almost day and night,
> especially in a place full of young people
> like here.

It is a gospel
about the future;
it is a gospel
about our hopes;
it is a gospel
about our expectations;
it is a gospel
about an issue
that can be seriously misunderstood.
> It is a gospel
> that can be explained in this way:
> that in so far as we are concerned,
> *nothing*
> will ever happen in this world
> at all!

Aren't we supposed to be
like that watchman:
waiting for his master?
> That watchman is, of course,
> taking care of his food
> every day,
> *while waiting for his Lord.*
> He washes, of course,
> his face every morning and every evening,
> *while waiting for his Lord.*

He is taking care of his health, of course,
from hour to hour,
while waiting for his Lord.
But for the rest:
no plans,
no activities,
nothing positive in view
of the coming of his Lord
in the end:
he is waiting only.
How often do we, Christians,
not compare
but too well
to that watchman?
We are waiting for the Lord
in the end;
we are quite willing to receive him
at the end;
we are keeping awake
until the end;
we are taking care of our food
—many of us even too well—
till the end;
we are washing ourselves
with very good soap
until the end;
we are taking care of our health
till the end,
    but for the rest:
    no plans,
    no activities,
    nothing positive in view
    of the coming of the Lord
    at that end.
Too many of us are waiting only,
some of us are even waiting prayerfully,
overlooking totally that the lord in the story
—even before addressing the watchman—
had been speaking to the other members of the household
indicating to each one of them their task.

If we expect Jesus
only in the end
then we are co-responsible
for Christ's absence
in this world
here and now.
The very absence Isaiah
was complaining about.
It is true that we should be waiting
for the return of Jesus,
but it does not follow
that we should sit down
idle
in view
of that coming.
It is correct to expect
that he will come
in the end,
but it does not follow
that he should be absent
therefore
from what we do now.
Jesus is not only coming
at the end of time.
He came to Mary
during her life
while she was barely sixteen years old
at the moment he was conceived in her womb.
He came to the apostles
in the middle of their lives,
calling Peter and John
away from their boats and their fish
and Matthew away from his cash register
and his coins.
Jesus does not come to us only
at the end of time.
He came to us
in baptism
or even before at the moment
we decided to be baptized.

We shouldn't be awake only in the end;
we should be awake
from minute to minute,
from hour to hour,
from day to day,
from week to week,
from month to month,
from year to year,
from decade to decade,
and together
from century to century.
We modern people
very often *think* and *reason*
that all can be computerized
and foreseen,
but we *believe*
something else.
We believe
that at any moment of the day
he can step into our lives,
again and again
inviting us
in the direction
of the ever rising and receding
promised land.

2.

GOD'S HOPE IN THIS WORLD

Mark 1: 1–8

The gospel by Mark
starts by saying:
"Good news about Jesus,"
but immediately after that trumpet blast
not Jesus,
but John the Baptist
is introduced to us.
     John in the wilderness,
     uncombed hair,
     in a set of skins,
     uncut nails,
     a very long uncontrolled beard,
     with the smell of the insects he used to eat
     all over him, and with a message
     of sin, repentance, and looming doom,
     that definitely did not mellow his voice
     notwithstanding the honey
     he ate.
Yet, even John was the bringer
of good news.
That must have been the reason that people came to him,

first one or two,
then some more
and finally hundreds and thousands,
Jesus included.
In the disastrous world
in which he lived
John preached hope to those
who were the cause of that disaster.
John said:
you are not bound up
by the world in which you live.
John said:
there is a power in you
with which you can escape
from that world,
overcoming it.
There is hope,
there is life.
There are at the moment
in our world
some very strange stories
about people who were so sick
that everybody around them
said:
you are going to die,
you are not going to make it,
you are hopeless,
your disease is terminal.
Doctors said so,
nurses said so,
surgeons said so,
relatives and friends said so.
Some of those people, however,
did not accept that verdict
of their environment.
They said:
we might be condemned
according to you;

we might have no hope
in your world;
let us try then
to get out of your world
to save ourselves.
They tried
and some succeeded.
There is the report of an American professor,
Joseph Chilton Pearce.
His rather young wife became pregnant,
but her pregnancy unleashed in her
also
an extremely malicious disease.
She suffered from cancer.
She was operated upon
again and again,
until the surgeons said:
this is the end,
the end of your road.
It was then
that she and her husband decided
to try to escape from the world
in which she was condemned to death.
They reasoned:
there is in every human organism,
in any living organism
the power to heal;
let us tap that power
     And they isolated themselves
     in a far-off farm,
     and they only spoke to each other
     about health,
     and they prayed,
     and they influenced each other
     only in a positive way,
     and they talked day and night
     about that possibility given with your body
     to heal,

and it was at the thirtieth day
that she suddenly felt
something happening in her
and she was healed.
She healed in the alternative world
they had constructed around themselves;
a world in which
she did not die.
    Would it not be possible
    to understand the message of John
    —that voice in the wilderness of our world—
    in that way?
You know
the enormous difficulties
under which we live.
We seem to be condemned to die
socially,
economically,
and family-wise
in a world
where uprightness,
honesty,
and integrity
do not seem to count
at all.
    You know how sick humanity is
    according to all kinds of diagnostics,
    so much so
    that in a diabolical way
    everything good
    seems to be turned into something
    very evil.
To give you one example only:
during the recent energy-exposition
here in town,
at the occasion of the international meeting
on alternative sources of energy,
some "sun-collectors" were shown.

In those collectors
aluminium foil is used
to catch the sunlight
in order to make your water boil
and your bread to be baked.
        It is one of those hope-giving developments
        in an energy-poor world,
            helping it to be a better place.
But did you know
that some are thinking
about a solar-collector
orbiting around the world
as a source of energy?
        And that others immediately
        got the idea
        of the military possibilities
        of such a collector
        to burn their enemies
        out of existence
        from the sky?
It is in this world of ours
that John's message gives
hope,
because preaching repentance,
he pointed at the possibility
in us
to change
and to change the world
with ourselves.
        An alternative is possible,
        a new humanity can be built,
        there is hope in our world:
        in Jesus
        God's hope entered
        this world.

3.

KNOWN AND UNKNOWN

John 1: 6–8, 19–28

Again he stands before us
in his camelskin
with that strange smell of his
around him.
A sign of protest,
a sign of hope,
a sign of our longing
for something new,
for something better.
     What he said
     rings true
     even after two thousand years.
     He said,
     most probably he shouted:
     "There stands among you,
     unknown to you,
     the one who is coming
     after me."
It is obvious
that Jesus is among us.
You can't turn on the radio,
without hearing about him.
You can't walk down a street
without meeting him:

because of the street preachers,
because of the church buildings,
because of the hymns,
boys and girls,
men and women
are humming or singing
in the bus,
on the street,
or in the train.
He is there all right:
"Jesus loves"
pinned on the blouse
of the hospital nurse.
"Jesus saves"
pasted on the rear window
of a dangerously driven *matatu.* *
He is there all right
among us,
in the midst of us,
and yet,
although his name
is splashed out
all over the place,
so little seems to have been worked out
in his name.
It seems that he remained hidden,
barren,
unfertile,
fruitless,
unfunctional
in this world.
Of course,
it seems
that he lives
in the hearts of many.
Some days ago
I picked up a leaflet:
"How to Get to Heaven from Africa."
The authors give that way to heaven,
they say.

The way is
according to them:

    —to realize that you are a sinner

    —to realize that because of sin,
      each of us, including you,
      deserves eternal death (hell)

    —to realize that God loved us so much
      that he sent his only Son Jesus Christ
      to suffer and to die in our place

    —to realize that Jesus Christ
      is the only way to heaven

    —to receive his gift of eternal life
      by simply asking him
      to save you

    —to pray,
      to read the Bible daily
      and to meet other Christians
      to encourage you on the way.

Would that really be all,
would that be the whole of the message?
What about the world,
what about the others?

    We ourselves came here together
    this morning
    because of him.

    We remember him,
    we celebrate him,
    we commemorate
    how he was foretold,
    how he was hoped for,
    how he was announced,
    how he was conceived,
    how he was born,
    how he was living,
    how he broke his bread,
    how he shared his wine,
    how he was arrested,
    how he was killed,
    how he was dead and buried,

how he rose from the dead,
how he appeared to them!
But would that be all?
Would that contain
the whole of his message?
What about the world,
what about the others?
We remember the past,
we are on the lookout
for the future,
but what about the
here and *now*?
What about the visions
of the prophets,
who saw,
as Isaiah in the first reading of today,
both
praise *and* integrity,
justice and peace
spring up
in the sight of the nations
here in this world
    as the earth makes
    fresh things grow,
    and as a garden
    makes seed spring up.
If you remain alone
—I am saved—
you remain
barren;
if you live only
in the past
you don't deserve
a place in the present.
    John said:
    there stands among you
    the one
    who is coming after me,
    unknown to you.

That is not true,
we know him,
we know his name.
And yet it is true.
Didn't he remain
a stranger to us,
in his aspirations
and in his plans?

matatu: small local buses, known for their reckless drivers.

4.

MARY'S VISION

Luke 1: 26–38

Mary
must have been
a very remarkable woman.
No wonder
she was his mother.
>She needed some time
>to understand
>what had happened to her.
>The earliest reports say
>that she was very confused initially
>and that
>—even in the presence of an archangel—
>she had some questions.
>But once she understood,
>she made her decision immediately.
She closed her curtains,
she closed her windows,
she closed her door,
she closed her house,
>not to lock herself up
>in it,

considering herself
as a kind of living tabernacle
with that treasure
in her womb,
putting so to speak
two candles and some flowers
in front of herself,
meditating day and night
about her privileged position.
No,
she closed her curtains,
she closed her windows,
she closed her door,
she closed her house
    to do something else:
    she went out
    to go to her aunt
    Elizabeth.
What had happened to her
was not going to be a private issue
only.
    When preparing this sermon
    I read several commentaries
    on this gospel.
    And very rightly so
    they all say
    that Mary gives us an example
    of how we should discern
    the Spirit of God in our lives.
    They all say
    that Mary gives us an example
    of how we should say "*yes*"
    to God's call in our lives.
Her "yes" was the beginning
of all and everything
that would happen to her
during the rest of her life.
Just like our "yes"
will be the beginning

of all and everything
that will happen
during the rest of our lives.
     Mary gives, however,
     a wider example.
     Mary is not trapped
     in that beginning.
     Mary does not restrict herself
     to those purely personal attitudes.
     Mary understood,
     as the angel had told her,
     that there was more, much more
     at stake.
Hadn't the angel
given that now growing person
in her womb,
the name JESUS,
meaning SAVIOR?
     Hadn't the angel spoken
     about a reign,
     his reign,
     that would last for ever and ever?
She must have been thinking
of all that,
the visions of the prophets
spinning in her head,
while she was walking
her long way
to her aunt Elizabeth.
She must have been thinking
of all that
while she saw the normal human scene
about her
in the streets and on the roads.
     Soldiers accompanying
     their Roman officers,
     chasing everybody else
     in the ditches alongside the road,
     to let those gentlemen pass.

The rich
full of contempt avoiding
to mingle with the poor.
>She herself,
>a poor up-country girl
>being pushed and looked at
>by men all around.
And then in the middle of the road,
with her savior in her womb,
with the prophets filling her head,
she suddenly got
that flash of insight.
>Before she reached her aunt
>she had understood
>what it would mean,
>that kingdom of his.
>She had suddenly understood
>what it meant that she
>—of all persons—
>was carrying the seed
>of all change
>in this world.
She had understood
that this would mean
a real new beginning
for all and everyone
and the end
of all that had and has power
in this world.
>Did she,
>seeing this,
>suddenly laugh
>aloud?
She was now at her aunt's house.
Elizabeth came out to greet her.
John in her womb gave her his push,
and Elizabeth cried out:
"What an honour that you came,
the mother of my Lord."

And all at once,
Mary,
who had had no one to talk to,
erupted in a vision
so wide
that she could not but sing:
> "Look at what happened to me,
> in me it is clear
> that God is going to change
> the whole order of things;
> it is through me
> that God showed
> that this world
> is going to change!"

Brother or sister,
that is what we should learn
today
from her.
God is not only going to change
private hearts;
God is not only to assure
peace of mind.
God is going to do all that
but only because
God is going to change
all structures
in this world,
> and when Mary said
> "*yes*"
> she did not only open herself
> to receive him in her womb;
> she opened herself
> to that vision
> as we should
> in all we do.

What she carried in her womb,
gave her a vision
wide as this world
and lasting like human history.

It is not for nothing
that she is called
the mother of all,
queen of the universe.

5.

THE ANGELS LEFT

Luke 2: 1–14

Luke does not mince
his words.
He makes one thing
very clear.
Jesus coming
is good news,
the devil and evil
fell from their throne
and the kingdom of God
has taken over.
      Take the story tonight.
      In Rome
      the emperor Caesar Augustus
      had issued a decree
      for the registration of the whole world.
      This registration was not
      a mere administrative matter.
      This registration was in order to be able
      to clamp down better
      on the colonialized peoples
      all over the world
      in view of the paying of tax,
      in view of the greed of the ruling elite.

Jude the Galilean
had organized an armed revolt
against this registration
but he had lost the battle
and that is why
Joseph and Mary
—notwithstanding Mary's condition—
had been forced
on the road.
Rome stood in the hearts and the minds
of the Jews
as the symbol
for all evil.
It is night
when the story starts,
a pitch-dark night.
In town the Roman census takers
were still bending
over their ledgers and books,
filling in the details.
Soldiers were patrolling the streets,
when in the open field
in a stable
Mary gave birth
to her child.
A child born out of people
without any importance,
up-country people,
victims of the rulers in town
and in the metropole Rome.
Announced by the kick of a son
in the womb
of an old barren woman
with a dumb-struck father,
born from the poor
and the helpless.
            And then those angels came,
            first one,
            then some,
            and finally a whole throng.

They did not go to those census takers,
they did not go to Herod
or the highpriests,
they did not even go to the monks
in the desert
to tell their news.
They went to the most marginal ones
in the neighborhood,
they went to the shepherds
considered by all,
the political,
the economical,
and the religious well-to-do's,
as scum,
as vermin,
as unclean.
The light of the angels
shone on them;
the heavenly songs
were heard by them;
the newness,
the alternative world,
the kingdom of God
started among them.
Luke does not mince
his words;
he makes one thing
very clear.
He makes Jesus play
his prophetic role
from his very birth,
from his cradle itself:
criticizing the old world
and its power,
introducing the new world,
the new society,
the new ethics,
the new human identity.
It was not only he
who was born that night.

It was a whole new world,
beginning not among those
operating and managing
the old order,
but emerging from its victims
in splendor and light.
      That is what Mary knew and felt.
      That is what Simeon and Anna foresaw.
      That is what the angels sang.
      After their song
      they left this earth.
      They must have thought
      that he together with us
      could be relied
      upon.
      Amen.

6.

BEYOND THE FAMILY CIRCLE

Luke 2: 22–40

That morning
Mary washed her baby Jesus
with extra care.
Joseph went out
to buy two turtledoves
for the sacrifice.
It was a very homely scene
those two caring for the third;
those two fulfilling together the law;
those two walking together
the considerable distance to the temple
with Jesus.
No wonder
that from days of old
pious authors
saw that family
as the model for all human families.
I don't want to be sarcastic,
but I wonder
whether that family
was not seen so easily
as a model for all

because we know so very, so very little
about them.
Did Joseph work at home
or was he an absentee male?
Did Mary stay the whole day
with Jesus
or had she to work
as a charwoman
with one of the richer families
in town,
in order to be able
to feed herself and Jesus.
We simply do not know.
We might dream
about the three of them
piously and comfortably
together
like we see them
on holy pictures,
and in the imagination of so many,
who believe
in the sanctity
—and rightly so—
of that family-type.
But what can you really do
with that model
when social and economic situations
make it impossible.
I know in this country
a priest sociologist
who started to study,
and to discuss with his people,
their family difficulties.
He had made the hypothesis
that those difficulties were all due
to the personal irresponsibility
of the fathers and mothers involved,
their drunkenness,
their faithlessness,

their adulterous promiscuity,
their lack of restraint,
their fickleness;
but doing his research
he had to change
his original assumption.
The real underlying reason
for most of the difficulties
was the situation
in which those people
were obliged to live.
Research at the University of Nairobi
proved
that 65 percent of the families in Kenya
are without the father at home.
That for that reason
and for some further reasons too,
70 percent of the men in Kenya
feel very frustrated
and non-participants
in their own society!
Not to speak about all the difficulties
of all those mothers,
and their children,
without their husbands,
without their fathers
at home.
How did those three
live?
Were they living in their own
house
or were they packed
together with two or three other families
in one small room
sleeping on their one bed
in turns?
Again, brother or sister,
I don't know,
but you don't know either.

One of the things we do know
is told us
today by Luke.
When Joseph and Mary
came to the temple,
they were met by two old people,
Simeon and Anna.
It is rather strange
that we don't hear anything
about the temple-officials
they must have met.
Not a word is mentioned
of what the priests said,
but what that old man
and that old woman said
was never forgotten.
Simeon said:
finally salvation,
salvation for all nations.
You see this child,
he is destined for the fall and the rising
of many;
destined to be a sign
that is rejected
so that the secret thoughts of many
will be laid bare.
Then that old lady Anna
took over,
and 84 years old
she too spoke
about the deliverance,
about the liberation
of Jerusalem.
Those two old people
praised Jesus,
they praised Mary,
they praised Joseph,
they praised that holy family
our model,

but they saw that family
and the relationships in that family
in view of greater things,
in view of a larger mission,
in view of the crisis,
      the change,
      the justice,
      the peace and the kingdom
      Jesus had come to bring.
Brothers and sisters
all the virtues
and love
necessary for a good family-life
are very often threatened
these days.
      Aren't they threatened
      because we don't see
      our families in the light
      of what Simeon and Anna
      said
      to Joseph, Mary, and Jesus?
      Aren't our families
      living under those threats
      because we in our families
      aren't sufficiently interested
      in that crisis,
        that change,
        that justice
        that peace and that kingdom
        he came to bring?

7.

MANY SAW BUT FEW FOLLOWED

Matthew 2: 1–12

Those wise men
who came to Jesus
did not profit
from any secret information
that made them move.
> They had seen a star,
> and stars are public things.
> Take the star that is nearest to us,
> the sun;
> such a star is so public
> that it affects the lives
> of all of us.
Though the star they followed
could be seen
and was seen by all,
those three only
decided to follow it.
> Traditionally it is said
> that they were three.

In fact we do not know
how many they were.
The only indication
to come to that number of three
is
that they unpacked
three gifts: gold,
              frankincense,
              and myrrh
when they arrived.
Maybe there were more
than three,
all carrying the same gifts,
maybe there were only two,
we don't know.
What we do know
is
that their number
was small, very small.
Not all who had seen the star
came,
only few, very few.
The others were so tied up
in their daily lives
that they saw the star
but they did not pay any further attention
to it at all.
          That was not necessarily
          because they were
          indifferent.
          I think that most of them
          were very aware
          of the type of life
          they were living.
          Most of them
          were very interested
          in a change,
          a radical change
          in their human lot.

But they must have thought
that their own personal experience,
that their own personal life,
that their own personal effort
could have no influence
in that change.
They lived such vague
and often ambiguous lives
that they could not see
where they ever
would be able to enter
into the thrust of human history.
>They were in a way
>non-participants.
>That is why they did not
>come.
Things like
history and destiny,
change and liberation,
salvation and redemption
were hanging as high above
their aspirations
as the star
was hanging above
their heads.
>Some, however, saw the star
>and they followed
>it.
>We don't know
>much about them;
>we do know
>that they related
>what they saw
>to human history
>and to God's presence
>in this world.
They were wise,
but hadn't the others been invited
to be wise too
by that star?

They were proved to be right.
When they arrived in Jerusalem
everything suddenly started to move.
It was at their arrival
that Jesus started to play his role
in human history.
Up to then
nobody had noticed practically
anything.
All had been going on
as if he had not come
at all.
Neither the king nor the priests
knew anything.
The angels had informed
the shepherds,
but what role do shepherds play
in human history?
Joseph and Mary
must have been in the temple
before those wise men came;
otherwise they would not have been obliged
to pay the sacrifice of the poor,
two turtle-doves,
after having received
the gold, the myrrh, and the frankincense.
     As Mary could not have gone to the temple
     before forty days after the birth had passed,
     the kings must have arrived
     more than six weeks
     after the birth.
All had remained peaceful.
Up to then
the official circles in town,
the politicians,
the priests,
the army officers,
and the press
did not know
a thing.

When those wise men arrived
the drama began,
the drama that would determine
the destiny of Jesus.
From the beginning
the scene
was set.
Men of goodwill
confronting the dark,
the lust, and the murder
of the men of evil will.
Herod planning
to kill
and Jesus
victorious.

> The prophecies
> were going to be fulfilled,
> the oldest ones
> and the most recent ones,
> those of Simeon and Anne,
> those of Elizabeth and Mary.

And it all started
because those wise men
had been willing
to take their own life-experience
seriously.
It all started
because they had been willing
to consider what happened to them
as a sign
of what would happen
to humanity
as such.

> They played their role,
> and doing that
> they made the crisis start,
> the crisis
> Jesus had brought
> into their lives
> and into their world.

We should be willing
to be wise like them.
We should be willing
to play their role.
We should be willing
not only to see,
but to follow that star
in our own lives.
We should be willing
not only to see,
but to follow that star
in our societies
and in our days.
Amen.

8.

JOHN'S ADDITION

Mark 1: 7–11

If John had been an ordinary man
he would not have been noticed.
He was no ordinary man,
he was extraordinary,
he was eccentric in his clothing,
           in his diet,
           in his manners,
           in his talk.
John was not only an eccentric;
if John had been a mere eccentric
nobody would have come to him
in the way people came to him.
       John was struggling with a problem,
       that was their problem,
       and that is why they came
       from all over.
Yesterday I was with some priests.
They were talking about preaching,
and one said:
as long as you have a clear opinion,
and you are convinced of it,
you stand personally behind it

42

and you deliver it
with that kind of conviction,
everyone will listen and profit.
That is not true,
another one said:
of course, that is not true.
They will listen only
when you are speaking about something
that does not only interest them,
but that bothers them,
that worries them,
that keeps them busy.
They come to listen only
when they suppose
that you can help them
a bit
in their own problems.
They are from that point of view
like a person with a terrible pain.
Such a person is not interested
in the finest food;
he is not interested
in the most honoring invitation;
he is not interested
in the richest diamonds;
he is not interested
in a full bag of gold;
he is interested only
in anyone
who can take away
the pain.
That was the reason
that they came to John.
He talked about something
they recognized;
he talked about something
that bothered them;
he talked in a sense
like they talked,

but he talked about it
with a difference.
> John was preaching
> about their situation;
> John was preaching about the situation
> in their world.
> John was complaining,
> John was criticizing,
> John was moaning,
> John was crying,
> John was upset,
> John was afraid,
> John spoke about doom,
> John spoke about a threatening collapse,
> John spoke as they spoke,
> John spoke as we speak
> about humanity,
> about the church,
> about the leadership,
> about politics,
> about the people around us.
They did not come
because John did only that.
They would not have come
if John had done only that.
He would not have been a help,
he would have been a repetition.
he would not have got them
out of their homes,
out of their bars,
out of their synagogues,
> where that criticism
> and that moaning
> was rampant.
John added something,
John changed something
John changed all.
John said:
there is hope.

John said:
you can change.
John said:
someone else
is going to come.

John pointed
in the middle of the darkness,
and the shadows of this world,
John pointed
in the middle of the negativeness
of their personal lives,
to the little light
still present,
to the positive
in them.
John gave them
hope.

That must have been the reason
that Jesus too
came to him.
Jesus did not come
to hear the laments;
Jesus did not come
to hear the moanings;
Jesus came
because of *the hope*
John spoke about.

That hope in itself,
that hope on its own
was already a new start,
the beginning
of an alternative world.

That is why he went to John,
that is why he stepped into the bitter water
of this world.
He bent his head,
John took his shell,
the cup or the saucer
he baptized with,

and suddenly that little light
in all of them,
that little hope,
>   burst into glory,
>   fire and flames:
>   heaven opened,
>   and while he stepped
>   out of the death,
> >   the darkness, and
> >   the bitterness
> >   of that water
>   a voice was heard:
>   *this is my son*,
>   and the new creation
>   started,
>   the new creation
>   started,
>   the new creation
>   started.
That newness will start in us,
that newness will start in the world,
not
when we are only moaning,
not
when we are only living in failure and guilt;
it will start in us
when we too
have sufficient hope
to see the light,
to see what Jesus saw:
that wavering flame in us
>   notwithstanding all the evil,
>   the limitations,
>   the darkness,
>   and the shadows
>   within and around us.
>   A flame he is not going to quench,
>   a flame he is willing to feed
>   for ever and ever.

9.

SIX IN ONE

John 1: 35–42

This week we start
the week of prayer for Christian unity.
I don't know whether the readings of this Sunday
have something to do
with those prayers.
Maybe they have.
In any case
they give a beautiful description
of six totally different people
who, though different,
had one thing in common,
their passionate interest
in the coming of the kingdom of God
here on earth.

> Samuel was about 12 years old
> when he was called.
> He was the helper and guide
> of the old prophet Eli
> who was losing his eyesight.
> Samuel was asleep when called.
> The sleep of a child
> in the beginning of the night.

The voice of God
had to call him four times
before he woke up
to its reality,
but once woken up
he said:
yes, here I am,
and he became a prophet so great
that no word of his
ever fell lost
on the ground.
The second person we meet
is Paul;
he was not asleep
and not a boy either.
He was seated on his horse
with, in his pockets,
the warrants to arrest
all Christians,
and in his eyes
a glow of hatred,
when lightning
or something like that
bolted him
from that horse.
He too heard that voice
saying:
"Saul,
why do you persecute me?"
And he asked in the blindness
that had struck him:
"Who are you?"
and the answer had been
"I am Jesus."
John the Baptist
was called to the work of a prophet
even before he was born
in the womb of his mother
whom he had kicked from within

when she met Mary
announcing the coming of Jesus
and his kingdom.
Andrew and John the apostle
did not hear the voice of God
directly,
it seems.
They were talking
with their master,
with their guru,
John the Baptist
when Jesus passed.
It was John who told them:
he is the lamb of God,
and they followed him
into his house
and they found
all they had been looking for.
Next morning Andrew
met his brother Simon,
and he told him:
we found the Messiah.
And when Simon was introduced
to Jesus
he immediately
got his new role,
being renamed
Cephas, Rock, Peter
by Jesus.
Six different persons,
six different calls
in the womb,
at the age of twelve,
later in life,
violently,
peacefully,
just like all of us
were called
in so many different ways.

Those six did not differ only
in the way they were called;
they differed also
in their contributions,
in their gifts,
in their tasks and their missions
in view of the kingdom of God.
Samuel prepared it,
but he never saw it.
John announced it;
he saw him
who came to bring it,
but at that sight
he did not even become his follower;
he withdrew,
his task was over.
Peter and Paul
were in a serious conflict
over it,
because they had so clearly
different ideas
about what that kingdom
meant.
Andrew was going to be killed
because of it
on one of his mission journeys
in Greece,
and John would die
a very old man
on his bed
—the only apostle who died
like that—
after having written
his gospel
and his visions
about the final end.
> Very different persons
> who at times must have been very surprised
> to find themselves together
> as they did,

called by God
in view of his work.
It is Paul
who in his letter of today
reflects upon this,
how they, how all of us
together
make up the body of Christ.
Later he would explain
how we should consider ourselves:
    one as the heart,
    one as the head,
    one as a foot,
    one as the liver,
    one as a hand
    forming all together
    the one body of Christ.
    We are not the same,
    we are different,
    we are meant to be different,
    equally contributing
    to that body of Christ.
It is in our days
that the Christian unity movement,
started so long ago,
seems to have come to an impasse.
Hopes which were once very high
seem to have been frustrated
very deeply.
Might it not be
that we have been looking
for the wrong unity,
trying to make all of us,
trying to make all of the communities
the head,
or the heart,
or the kidneys?
    Haven't we been trying to be *one*
    in the externals,
    in the concrete applications,

manifestations,
and experiences
of our attachment to the Lord and his kingdom,
overlooking
that attachment
itself?
Let us try to look
for the unity
that bound the six of today
together:
their fidelity
to Jesus Christ,
their fidelity
to his Spirit of love,
and one day
we suddenly will see:
we formed his body
already long ago
together!
There is at least one place in this world
where a beginning
has been made
to realize that type of unity
at Taizé in France,
where monks from different Christian traditions
live together
in a real catholicity.
In 1981
they organized a pilgrimage
to London
to celebrate together with others
our unity,
and more than 40,000 young people
came together
to join them
in churches otherwise
practically empty.
Their presence
was a sign,

a writing on the walls
that still separate
us,
though being in the same house
and living
the same life.

10.

A TOTAL OVERHAUL

Mark 1: 14–20

Jesus started his preaching.
He could not postpone
any further.
John had been arrested,
he had to step in his place,
he had to take up the task
assigned to him.
He went to Galilee
and he started to speak.
What he said
seemed to be simple.
He said:
"The time has come,
the kingdom of God is at hand,
repent
and believe the good news."
His preaching is not in vain.
His words do not fall on the ground
without bearing fruits.
Several people hearing his voice
and his message
leave everything
to follow him.

54

Some are mentioned:
Andrew, James, John,
Simon.
> Within a few days
> it was clear
> that the old world
> was disappearing
> and that a new world
> was coming.
> The expectancy
> turned into fulfillment;
> the hope
> into excitement.
> The world as they knew it
> was passing away,
> all problems
> would be tackled,
> all issues
> solved.

That was 2,000 years ago
among totally different people
in a foreign culture,
in a very small group
of the world's population.
> It is touching to see
> how their excitement
> spilled over
> into our days.
> It is wonderful
> that the story is still
> told.
> *But are not all fairy tales*
> *that way,*
> *are not all nursery rhymes*
> *immortal?*

How can we take
in all earnestness
that type of preaching
seriously
in our days

at a university
among scholars
in between our research
and lectures,
our analyses of the situation
and our project-planning?
How would we be able
to take that simple message:
        "The kingdom is at hand,
        repent
        and believe the good news!"
as a tool
for all the work
that should be done
to solve
        our social,
        our medical,
        our economic,
        our scientific
        and our logistical problems?
What can we do
with those words
in view of food,
in view of water,
in view of security,
in view of the population problems,
in view of the refugees,
in view of the exploitation of people and nature
all around us?
        It is nice to think
        about Jesus,
        it is nice to dream
        of Jesus,
        it is nice to pray
        to Jesus,
        it is nice to see films
        on Jesus,
        it is nice to have a picture
        of Jesus,

it is nice to write
Jesus' name
on walls and on carbumpers,
but isn't all this at the same time
rather naive and childish,
perplexing and bewildering?
What did he mean?
What can he mean to us?
What did he want?
What did he want from us
in our modern days,
when we seem to be at the point
of solving all our problems
rationally and scientifically?
Isn't that
what we are taught
not only at this university
but at all universities
and schools?
It is only a question
of a better analysis,
more correct statistics,
a more integrated interdisciplinary approach
and a few more seminars,
workshops, conferences,
symposia, and congresses.
I met once here
a lecturer at the Faculty of Commerce,
an American,
who said
that he too was waiting
for a new world,
and he added:
it will come
when we have it all reasoned out
and computerized.
What did Jesus
know about all this
in his time

in that tiny part of the world,
Galilee?
    No wonder
    that people laugh at us,
    his followers,
    saying
    that we are misfits,
    reactionary,
    stupid,
    old-fashioned,
    blind, fruitless,
    and dry.
And yet, brothers and sisters,
the more science progresses,
the more technology
dazzles us
with its tremendous developments,
the more we might notice
that something seems to be lacking.
All those developments
do not seem to be only a blessing
but also a threatening curse.
    It is as if something is missing,
    the right direction,
    the right intention,
    the right meaning,
    an underlying principle.
It is in that context
that the message of Jesus of today
does count
and does count very heavily.
    The time has come,
    he said,
    the kingdom of God
    is close at hand,
    repent
    and believe the good news.
That was the start,
but he showed later
what he meant.

He showed
that it is possible
that a human being
can live with a changed heart,
with an outgoing love,
interested in the welfare
of all human life
around him.
      He showed
      that this love will work out
      healing and restoration,
      fulfilment and invigoration.
He showed
how God's gifts to us,
science and technology included,
should be used
to the benefit of all.
      He showed
      how we can break through sin and greed,
      through ignorance and stupidity,
      through egoism and shortsightedness.
He showed
how the direction of the human will
can be changed
through the power of God.
      It is that *possibility*
      of repentance
      and a change
      that is good news indeed
      for the whole of humankind.
It is the start
of a total overhaul,
the beginning of God's kingdom on earth,
a changed human life.

11.

DID HE WANT TO BE CLEANSED?

Mark 1: 21–28

He was in the synagogue.
He was preaching.
They had heard so many sermons
in their lives before.
They had heard so many
that they knew the themes by heart.
They had heard so many
that they had categorized them
in their heads;
they had heard so many
that they asked themselves
which sermon would it be today,
sermon A,
sermon B,
or sermon C.
> Most probably he chose
> a text from scripture.
> They knew the text.
> They knew its setting.
> They knew what could be said
> about that text.

It had been said
a hundred times before,
over and over again.
All had been fixed
long ago.
All that preaching
had never done very much good,
nor very much harm.
The good ones
remained mediocre
and the evil ones
remained evil.
No one ever felt
particularly challenged.
Jesus had taken an old text,
true,
but he did not stick
to the old theme;
he went far beyond that,
he told them things
they had never heard before
      and the good ones admired
      his power
      but the evil ones
      were challenged too.
There was that man
in the crowd
with an evil spirit.
Most times it is suggested
that the man was possessed
by the devil.
But, maybe, the evil spirit of that man
was not an alien,
a foreigner,
a stranger,
or someone different from him.
      It might have been
      that he himself
      had been wrapped up
      in himself.

It might have been
that he himself
was a glutton, a thief,
an exploiter, or a selfish egoist.
He started to shout.
It might have been
that the devil shouted
from within him,
but maybe it was not the devil,
but he himself
who shouted,
understanding what Jesus said,
understanding what Jesus asked,
objecting to it.
   He understood
   that believing Jesus
   meant changing your life
   and he did not want to do
   that at all.
He understood
that he was not the only one
living uncleanly in corruption.
   He understood
   that corruption and deceit
   was the structure
   on which the whole of the world relied
   and he shouted
   —like all the others around him
   would say later:
   if we allow
   that change to take place;
   if we permit
   Jesus' way;
   if we start to realize
   his vision,
   our whole world
   is going to collapse
   around us.
He did not like the idea,
he did not see it as a good thing,

he did not want to be cleansed,
he objected:
"What do you want with us,
Jesus of Nazareth?
You have come to destroy
us!!"
     But Jesus said sharply:
     "Be quiet!
     Come out of him!"
And the man got convulsions,
he shook and he vibrated,
he shuddered and he trembled,
he shouted and he cried.
     No wonder:
     just think about yourself;
     would not all your limbs
     shake,
     when evil would be torn
     from them?
Suddenly the convulsions
stopped.
He was free.
He left the synagogue
a totally different man,
free of the devil,
free from evil.
     Would we like to change
     as he did?
     Would you like,
     really and sincerely,
     to change
     as he did?
     Would you like to have evil
     driven out of you
     completely,
     would it not destroy
     your world?
Do we really mean that prayer
during Mass
when we say:

"Deliver us, Lord,
from every evil;
keep us free from sin."
Do you?
    And yet
    it is in that way only
    that his kingdom
    in us
    and in this world
    can start.

12.

WORK NOT DONE

Mark 1: 29–39

That day he healed *many*
implying
that he didn't heal them *all*.
Why didn't he heal all?
Why doesn't he heal all?
     He had been in the synagogue,
     he had been heard preaching in a new way,
     he had been seen chasing out evil
     and now he was on his way
     to the house of his friend Simon.
When he arrived
he was told
that Simon's mother-in-law
was in bed,
with a very serious fever.
That fever was not only serious
because her temperature
was so high;
her sickness was so grave
because this
"fire in the bones"
was considered by everyone
as a punishment from God.

65

Did the book Leviticus not read:
"I will punish you
with wasting and fever
to dim the eyes
and sap the life" (26:16)?
> Without any further nonsense
> Jesus went to her;
> there were no strange words,
> there were no secret manipulations,
> there were no incantations,
> there were no extra prayers,
> there was not even the suspicion of magic:
> he just took her hand
> and helped her up.
> She got rid of her fever
> and she started to serve them.
As long as her body
had been racked by that fever
> one minute cold,
> one minute burning,
> one minute freezing,
> one minute scalding,
she was to the bystanders
the example of one
under the influence of evil.
> Now, healed,
> she became the example
> of one touched by Jesus:
> starting to serve them,
> starting to serve God
> immediately.
In the meantime evening had fallen;
it was the end of a sabbath day.
During that day
nobody had been allowed to walk,
except to and from the synagogue,
but now they were allowed to walk
and notwithstanding the falling dark,
they came from all sides,

the whole town came out
with all their sick
and evil spirits,
> and he healed,
> and he healed,
> and he healed
> as many as he could
> before night had fallen
> in total dark
> and people had to leave.
The end of the first day
of his "public" life
in the gospel of Mark!
He went to sleep,
but very early in the morning
he came out of his bed,
he went off to pray.
> While he was doing that
> those in Capernaum
who had not been healed
the night before
came out of their beds too
heading for the house
where they were staying.
> They woke Simon,
> they asked him for Jesus.
> Simon could not find him;
> his blanket lay folded
> in the corner where he had slept.
> Together with some others
> he went to have a look
> for him.
Finally they found him
in prayer,
They told him:
everybody is looking
for *you*.
> But he answered:
> let us go,

let us go elsewhere
so that I can preach;
that is why I came.
And though they heard
the noise of the crowd around the house
increase
and although they saw
all kinds of people
on their way to that house,
they did not return;
they left
to those other places.

He left the work
at Capernaum *undone*
at least in so far as those sick
around that house
thought.
Just as he left the work,
even at the end of his life,
after the resurrection,
undone
in so far as his disciples and followers
thought.

He left
promising to come back,
but up to now
he has not returned.
He left his work
uncompleted,
he left us partly
in the dark,
he left us in expectation,
he left almost all issues
in a sense totally open,
he left so much to us.
Because that is what he did
before he left them;
he told them:

"You saw me,
I enlightened your path,
I got you out of your stupor,
I got you out of your paralysis,
I got you out of your blindness,
I got you out of your deafness,
I got you free from 'the fire in your bones,'
I got you free from evil spirits,
    so now
    I am sending you,
    it is your turn,
    you should do it!"
    And we should!
Sometimes you hear Christians say
that all is over,
and in a sense it is,
because he broke through it all.
But he said
that what was possible for him
would be possible for us
and he sent us
on our way
to be like him
and serve;
    to be like that mother-in-law of Simon
    who was healed,
    who came from her bed
    and who immediately
    related in a new way
    to him
    and to the whole of humanity.
    Don't you think
    that she served those sick
    around her house
    after he had left?
    Of course she did!
We often say
he came to save us,

and that is true,
but it is not all.
He will walk away from us
in the dark of the night
to pray,
to pray for us
so that we might save
just as he did.

13.

NOT LIKE A TANK
ON ITS COURSE

Mark 1: 40–45

The gospel story today
is so typically a Jesus story
that we might overlook
that the story of Jesus
and that loquacious leper
is a tale we all know
from our own lives.
      You all know
      —unfortunately—
      what a tank is.
      It is that kind of iron vehicle
      that is armoured all over,
      that has all its windows and doors shut,
      and that bulldozes its way
      through all and everything
      ruthlessly and blindly
      with a big, shooting gun
      on top.
A tank is definitely
a sign of strength;

71

it is a monument to power,
but a destructive one.
> You all know
> how certain people seem
> to live like tanks.
> They do not pay any attention
> to things that are going on around them.
> They have isolated themselves
> on their inner and on their own course,
> and they go their way
> without pity
> or restraint.
You all know
that each one of us
is now and then
like such a tank.
You know of yourself
how you acted
as if you did not hear
while the voice of another was pleading.
You know of yourself
how you acted
as if you did not see
when that hand was outstretched to you.
You know of yourself
how you did not stop
while someone else
was in dire need of you.
You remained strong,
because you said to yourself:
let me not become soft.
> And I think
> that—in a way—
> you were right,
> very right.
> If you had stopped,
> if you had seen,
> if you had listened,
> if you had not been strong,

you would have lost
most probably
a great deal.
Wasn't that the problem
Jesus seems to face
in the story of today?
There was that man
who blocked his way,
pleading on his knees
in front of him.
He said:
"Please, if you want to,
you can cure me!"
And a voice in Jesus
must have said:
don't do it,
he will tell all the others
and there will be no end
to your trouble.
You will have no rest
any more.
You will get so well known
that you won't be able
to drink a cup of water
alone,
ever.
Don't give in,
don't get soft,
be strong,
close up,
don't see,
don't hear!
But he did see
and he did hear
and he had pity on him
and he said:
of course,
I want you to be cured,
and he stretched out his hand,

and he touched the sick skin of that man,
and he spoke the words: be cured,
and the leprosy left him
there and then,
he was cured.
And then Jesus added
to make up for his lack of strength,
to make up for his weakness,
to protect himself:
don't tell any one!

He knew it would be in vain
because everyone who had known the man before
would ask him:
what happened to you,
what happened to your sickness?
What was he going to tell
them?
It was that weakness in Jesus
that made him deliver himself
continuously
to the people around him.
It was that weakness in Jesus
that made him find
the real center of his interest
always outside of himself.
It was always his Father,
it was always the other in need,
he never acted like
a closed-up, fire-spitting tank.
He always used his power
in view of others.
He loved,
and anyone who loves
puts himself or herself
in a very vulnerable position.

No wonder that one day
his family forced even his mother
to go with them
to tell him to get back home.

You are mad,
they told him,
ravingly mad,
get home.
It was that weakness in Jesus
that brought him in the final instance
to the cross
as Paul wrote
in his second letter to the Corinthians:
it was because of his weakness
that he was put on the cross (13:4)
but he added:
"It is through God's power
that he lives."
It was this weakness
that constituted his *love*,
his outgoing love
that made him identify
with the sick,
the hungry,
and the beaten-up ones.
If Jesus could see
(and through our eyes he sees it)
the situation in which so many of us
try to survive,
he would be moved by pity
(as we should be moved by pity).
A pity that would not only cause in him
feelings of warmth and care,
of submission and sympathy,
of meekness and forgiveness
but also of anger and shock
of resistance and a working
for justice at all cost.
The weakness that brought him
to the cross
is the only power
that can help us
in this world,

and we are asked,
we are invited
to participate in it
wholeheartedly,
notwithstanding the risks
involved.
Don't clatter through life
like a tank;
he didn't do that
either.

14.

JESUS THE MENACE

Mark 2: 1–12

Jesus had come back to Capernaum.
People came from all over to see him.
This time he was preaching to them,
he was explaining to them
what he thought and felt
about the world,
about God,
and about humankind.
     It is obvious
     from the gospel report
     that not all of them
     had just come
     to sit at his feet
     and listen,
     to swallow
     all he said.
     There were some sitting there,
     some scribes and also some others,
     who were listening to him
     very critically
     and who were making objections
     every time

when he seemed to contradict
their own set traditions.
He was doing that.
If he had not done that
they would not have come to listen.
If he has talked
as they talked
their god-and-man language
he would not have been a danger
to them at all.
But here was one
who from the first time
that he had opened his mouth
in the synagogue
had been speaking
in a way different from them,
with a new type of authority.
That must have meant
that he questioned and criticized
what they were accustomed to say.
It meant also
that he foresaw
something new
and that is exactly
what they could not
and would not
admit.
So they had come
to question him,
to heckle him,
to harass him,
to try to get him
to contradict himself;
defending their own position,
killing his influence
and the hope his listeners had,
that maybe
all might change.

As he was discussing with them,
he was not healing that day.
He was indoors
and the theological disputes about doctrine
seemed endless,
especially to those
who had come
with their sick.
They got impatient outside.
They were not interested
in all that talk
about the possibility of
a new world
and a new order of things.
They were interested
in that new world
here and now,
there and then.
They were interested
in healing.
Their impatience grew
and as they saw no chance
of getting near to him
through the door
or through the windows
they climbed on the roof,
they uncovered it,
and without any learned preambles
they lowered in front of him
the most concrete and urgent item
that exists in this world:
a human being in pain.

Suddenly the dispute
about the possibility
of the end to the old
and the beginning of the new
between him and his opponents
fell silent.

In that silence
they all looked
at that stretcher
with that man
in a few rags,
with his body falling apart
and its two piercing eyes
that asked for help,
that asked
to get rid of the old,
to get rid of the present
and to start
anew.
Asking to fulfill
the possibility,
they had said
he was not even allowed
to talk about.
> Jesus too looked at him
> and then he said
> in the continued silence:
> "My son,
> your past is done with,
> your sins are forgiven!"
A murmur went round,
their anger flared up,
he had *done*
what they did not even allow him
to talk about.
He had changed it all,
all bonds fell away.
The established order
—established by them—
broke up
under their eyes.
> But did it really?
> Was, what he had said,
> not only bluff,

unforgivable and blasphemous bluff,
words in the air,
threatening
but for the rest
meaningless?
He looked at them,
they looked at him.
Did he smile?
I do not know.
He had guessed
their reaction;
he did not guess,
he *knew*,
and he said:
Why do you have those thoughts
in your hearts?
Which of these is easier,
to say to the paralytic
your sins are forgiven
or to say
get up,
pick up your stretcher,
and walk.
But to prove to you
that the son of man
has authority on earth
to forgive sins
—and now he turned to the man
on the stretcher—
"I order you,
get up,
pick up your stretcher
and walk,
go home!"
And to the horror
of those scribes
and to the joy
of all the others,

the old world
folded up
and a new one
was born:
the man stood up
from his stretcher
and walked
into the light
of a totally
new day!!

15.

FORTY DESERT DAYS

Mark 1: 12–15

Last Wednesday we started Lent.
The flowers we used last year
on Palm Sunday
to applaud Jesus
were burnt to ashes
the day before.
> Our resolutions,
> the ones we made
> to be with Jesus
> when we were waving
> those branches last year,
> had been burned
> to ashes
> long ago.
We put those ashes,
bitter,
salt,
and coarse
as they were,
on our foreheads
to show
that we had been unsuccessful,

83

to show
that we hope to do better,
and we started
our period of Lent,
we started to do penance;
and in the gospel of today
we appeal
to the forty days of Jesus
in the desert
to explain to ourselves
what we do.
>It is right to appeal
>to that period in the life of Jesus
>on condition
>that we really know
>what he did
>there in the desert
>and on condition
>that we are willing
>to follow his example,
>opening up to what the Spirit
>worked out in Jesus
>during that period
>of his life.
It seems to me
that we often
very conveniently overlook
what happened to him.
We overlook
because like in so many spiritual affairs
we remain the children
we were long ago.
>We are quite willing to do
>some penance, we say.
>Some of us decide
>to drink less,
>to smoke less,
>to eat less,
>to spend less,

to give to the poor,
to visit the sick,
to pray a bit more,
and all those resolutions
are excellent
and they all have something to do
with what Jesus did,
but it all remains
at a childlike level.
What Jesus underwent
was different.
Mark is short
about it,
but he says
everything to be said.
Jesus was sent into the desert
by the Spirit,
by the Spirit of God.
That must have been
a terrific experience
just imagine
that you were taken up
by the Spirit of God!
That Spirit of God
chased him into the desert.
He did not go there,
he was driven;
and once in the desert
a fight developed,
a very fundamental fight,
a basic fight,
the fight with all the evil
in this world.
The way in which Mark
indicates and characterizes
that fight
is outdated,
it is a bit primitive.
It does not appeal to us.

Even the number 4 in 40
is an indication
of what happened.
Forty days,
ten times four,
four was the number
that stood for *the earth*
with its four basic elements
      earth,
      air,
      water, and
      fire.
There is the image of
the wild animals,
and all those elements and animals
are described
as beings
ruled by Satan,
the enemy,
the adversary.
      The fight is won
      by him.
      That is why,
      when coming out,
      he can proclaim
      the good news from God:
      the time has come,
      the kingdom is close at hand,
      repent
      and believe.
It is at this point
that we come in.
Those words are
addressed to us.
We should not only look
at his past
in that desert;
we should look
at ourselves

in the present
and join Jesus
in his cosmic struggle.
            All this can be said
            in another way:
            it is in that desert,
            in that wilderness
            with those animals,
            with those elements
                —and the angels
                assisting him—
            that Jesus entered
            as an active participant
            in the history of humankind,
            humanity
            on its way
            to itself
            and to God.
We are invited
during this Lent
to enter into that history too,
to participate
in that fight.
Amen.

16.

FROM IMPOSSIBLE TO POSSIBLE

Mark 9: 2–10

One of the reasons
that they followed him
must have been
their sense of powerlessness.
They knew
that they would not be able to do
anything
by themselves
about the world
in which they lived
and about the lives
they were living.
>They were like that soldier
>in that very old Asian story
>who had looted a town.
>He was trying to sell
>an exquisite rug,
>one of the spoils.
>"Who will give me
>a hundred shillings
>for this carpet?"

he shouted all through town,
once home again
from his venture.
He found an eager buyer
in no time.
After the sale
a bystander,
aware of the value of the rug,
approached the seller
and asked:
"Why did you not ask more
for that priceless rug?"
"Is there any number
higher than one hundred?"
asked the seller.
His conception
limited
his awareness
and his action.
Their conception of themselves
limited
their awareness
and their action.
It restricted even their awareness
of what he, Jesus,
might be able to do.
They had some hope
in him,
that is true,
but they had no idea
what they were really
in for.
That is why
he took them
with him
out of this world,
out of the world
they knew so very well,
out of the relations
they were accustomed to,

away from the water
they had been practically
living in.
      He took them with him
      to the top of the mountain
      and once up there,
      he started to change,
      first his clothing,
      but then he himself,
      transparent and yet opaque,
      white and yet full of color,
      and heavenly beings appeared,
      Elijah and Moses,
      and a discussion was held
      in which they heard him
      discuss with them
      the coming change,
      the pass-over,
      a transformed world.
They did not know
what to say,
they were taken
by surprise.
They mumbled something
about staying there
and about a tent or three.
      And then,
      to top it all,
      a cloud came down,
      a shadow fell,
      and a voice was heard:
      "This is my son,
      the beloved one,
      listen to him."
Suddenly all seemed over,
he was standing there again
as they had seen him
so often before,
one like them.

Now they knew
what they were in for,
not only he,
but they, themselves also:
had he not always been
like them;
had they not always been
like him?
He told them not to tell
what had happened to him
or
what would happen to them
before that new life
had risen
from the tomb
of the old.

And though they did not yet understand,
they looked at their hands,
they looked at their feet,
they looked at each other,
they looked at themselves
and they knew
that the power of change
would be given to them.
They knew
that they would be able to do more
than they ever expected to do.
So should we,
seeing ourselves reflected
in the image
of his transformed self:
Emmanuel, God with us.

17.

THE SIGN GIVEN

John 2: 13–25

He had overcome the temptations
so common and normal
in their and in our world.
He had shown
in himself
the brightness
of our real human possibilities,
the possibility of a change,
the possibility of a pass-over,
the possibility of a new human life.
> That morning he entered the temple,
> the center of their religious life,
> the center of their old religious life,
> a temple of stones,
> of gold and silver,
> a temple of sacrificed animals,
> of dying bullocks, of butchered pigeons,
> a temple against which
> —in the name of God—
> the prophets had been shouting:
>> "The Lord says:
>> Do you think I like all those sacrifices
>> you keep offering to me?

I have more than enough
of the sheep
you burn as sacrifices.
I am tired of the blood of bulls
and sheep
and goats.
Who asked you to do all this
when you come to worship me?
Who asked you to do all this tramping about
in my temple?
It is useless to bring your offerings.
I am disgusted with the smell of the incense
you burn.
I can't stand your new moon festivals,
your sabbaths,
and your religious gatherings;
they are all corrupted by your sins.
I hate your feastdays and your holidays,
they are a burden
that I am tired of bearing.
When you lift your hands in prayer
I won't look at you.
No matter how much you pray,
I will not listen,
for your hands are covered with blood.
Wash yourselves clean.
Stop all the evil
that I see you doing.
Yes, stop doing evil
and learn to do right.
See that justice is done,
help those who are oppressed.
Give orphans their right
and defend the widows.''
He had told them
that he had come to fulfill
the prophecies.
If so,
hadn't he to stop
the temple service?

That is what he did!
It was that morning
not only a question
of chasing those bankers and merchants
away;
it was that morning
not only a question
of letting those animals and birds
loose;
it was that morning
not only a question
of clearing the temple
of silver and gold.
What he did went much deeper,
what he did was more fundamental,
what he did was to stop a temple-service
that had outlived its aim
and that was no longer faithful
to its vocation.
Those present
must have known this.
That is why they asked:
"What sign can you show us,
authorizing *you* to do these things?"
It was as if they had expected
this end
any day,
but who was *he*
to terminate
it all?
He did not give them the sign
they asked for.
He had given them that sign
already:
the old temple-service
had been stopped
by him,
and the new temple
had been announced:

the one in which God is
with the orphans
and the widows,
with the sinners and the sick
forming
through Christ
one body,
God's temple
with us.

18.

EVIL UNDONE

John 3: 14–21

Nicodemus
must have been an old man,
a wise man with grey hair and a long white beard.
He had been hearing about Jesus,
he had seen him from a distance,
he had heard how Jesus
fought against all kinds of injustices,
how he defended the poor,
how he healed the sick,
how he protected children,
and he had started to like Jesus very much.
That is why he had made an appointment with him
that night.
He wanted to speak to Jesus,
he wanted to warn him
because he knew too
how people were trying to catch him.

> Jesus had accepted the invitation.
> It was night when they met.
> After having greeted each other,
> after having talked about the usual things,
> and after having sipped from their first glass of wine,
> Nicodemus had come to his point.

First he had sent everybody else away from the room,
he had checked that nobody was listening behind the door
or next to the window.
And then he had asked Jesus about his intentions.
What did he really want to do?
Should he not be much more careful,
did he not realize that he was making very many enemies,
the priests he had been telling the truth
and all the others,
he had been accusing of injustice and corruption?
Did he not know that if he went on like that
in his fight against evil and sin,
that he would be arrested,
that he would be harassed,
that he would be killed
and forgotten?
Would it not be better
if he did things more slowly?
What was the use of being a blazing piece of fireworks
to disappear in the dark,
leaving no hope
and making things consequently worse?
Was it really possible
to make everything new?
Had the things he, Jesus, had done
been wise:
healing on the sabbathday,
defending an adulterous woman,
upsetting the service in the temple?
Should he not restrict himself
to some more preaching,
to some more praying,
to some more consoling and comforting words?
   Jesus had listened to the old man
   full of respect;
   he must have been touched by his care,
   by his interest in him;
   he must have understood
   that Nicodemus meant very well,

that what he said was based
on a very long experience with life,
on a deep insight in human affairs.
But then he answered
and he said:
The son of man
—and he meant himself—
must be lifted up,
and he meant:
the son of man must be lifted up on the cross.
He explained to Nicodemus that he knew perfectly well
what would happen to him.
He told Nicodemus that he knew
that he would be arrested and tortured
and finally murdered.
But he added that
the cross was the only way out,
that it was the only way
by which humanity could be saved,
that it was the only way
of overcoming evil and sin,
corruption and injustice.
That is difficult to comprehend.
It was difficult to Nicodemus,
it is difficult to us.
Let us try to see
what Jesus meant.
To understand this
let us go to the night of his arrest.
It was dark in that garden
where he had been praying.
Suddenly there was a noise at the entrance of the garden,
policemen and soldiers,
with sticks, knives, spears, and swords
entered almost tumbling over each other.
They had been ordered by their paymasters
—the civil authorities,
the ecclesiastical leaders,
and some other locals,

who saw Jesus as a threat to the existing order
of which they profited so much
at the cost of so many—
to arrest Jesus.
He went up to them,
and when he was standing in front of them
he asked:
whom are you looking for,
whom are you coming to arrest?
They said:
Jesus of Nazareth,
and he said:
that is me,
but suddenly a terrific power came out of him
and they were all caught by that power
and they all fell flat on their faces in the mud.
When they got up again
wiping the mud out of their eyes and noses
they heard him ask again:
whom did you come to arrest,
and when they answered:
Jesus of Nazareth,
again that power went out of him
and again they fell to their horror
on their faces
in the mud,
and they must all have been cursing the moment
that they had decided to come,
leaving their wives and their children at home
near the fire.
But again they scrambled to their feet
and when he asked them for the third time,
whom are you looking for,
they answered him with very small and very thin voices.
Jesus,
and it was then,
but only then,
after having shown them his power,
that he *freely* delivered himself into their hands,

and they took him,
and you know what happened to him,
you know how they beat him up,
you know how they spat at him,
you know how they ridiculed him,
you know how they tortured him,
crowning him with thorns,
you know how they let him drag his cross to Calvary
and how they crucified him,
you know how they elevated him on the cross,
and how he died.
He delivered himself to evil,
he delivered himself to sin,
he delivered himself to injustice,
he delivered himself to corruption,
he stood on the side of all those who ever suffered
throughout human history
in view of goodness, justice, and peace.
The gospel tells us
how after his death
Nicodemus was among those
who came to bury him.
Nicodemus must have been telling the others
about that night
that he had been warning him
that he would be murdered
if he were not more prudent.
Brother or sister,
we know better.
We know how God, his Father and Mother,
raised Jesus from the dead
after three days.
After three days in the tomb
he was again with them,
showing that in his fight with evil,
not *evil*,
but *he*, Jesus, had won,
showing how sin had lost its power,
how injustice would be overcome.

That is what we should know
when we look at him on the cross,
seeing him bleed to death,
because of the evil in this world,
but knowing
that he overcame death
and all evil.
We should not only look,
we should not only say:
"We are washed in the blood of the lamb,"
with tears in our eyes
and pleasant feelings in our hearts,
we should *do* more.

Before he left them for good
he had told them:
"As I was sent,
I am sending you!"
We should join him
in his fight with evil
and sin
in ourselves
and in the society in which
we live and work.
That is what we should do,
that is what I should do,
that is what you should do,
finding your strength to do it
looking at his cross
and knowing about his victory.

19.

THE END OF THE CIRCLE

John 12: 20–33

It started very simple.
There were those Greeks
at the festival.
They went to one of his followers,
Philip,
to ask him
to introduce them to Jesus.
In fact they asked him for more,
they wanted to "see" Jesus
and experts tell us
that this meant
in the language of their time
that they wanted to be with him.

> Philip must have looked at them,
> those strangers,
> exotically dressed,
> speaking with a different accent,
> eating other food
> and consequently even smelling differently,
> with some apprehension.

He hesitated,
and not wanting to make a decision alone,

he went to Andrew
to explain.
> Would it be a good thing
> to hand on their message?
> Would it not be a precedent?
> Would it not be the end
> of their rather secure ethnic life together?
> What if all kinds of people
> were taken up in their circle?
> Did those others not do everything
> in another way?

Finally they went to Jesus
to explain to him the issue,
> > their hesitations,
> > and their doubts.

Should the circle
be broken up?
Should their approach
change?
> Jesus did not answer their question,
> it seems,
> because he neither said "yes,"
> nor did he say "no."

And yet he answered it,
but at a much more profound level,
at a level
where everything,
his whole life,
was at stake.
> He answered them
> by giving them an insight
> into his own feelings,
> hesitations, and decisions.
> He answered them
> by making them participate
> in that monologue,
> or dialogue
> he had been having
> already for quite some time,

and especially over those last days
at the festival.
Philip and Andrew
came to ask him
whether their circle and company
should not remain unchanged
notwithstanding the request
of those Greeks.
He, himself,
was struggling with the question
whether or not all should change.
    Shouldn't the life
    he had been living
    be given up?
    Shouldn't the life
    they had been living together
    be broken up
so that a new life
would be able to begin:
a new era,
a new perception,
a new morality,
a new everything.
    Shouldn't the grain
    that existed and lived
      —restricting that life
      to its narrow confinement—
    fall in the ground,
    break and die,
    giving new life?
He was dialoguing with himself
when he said:
now the hour has come,
and
how troubled is my heart;
and
shouldn't I ask my Father
to excuse me,

and
but didn't I come precisely
because of this hour?
>Shouldn't he do
>what he had been tempted to do,
>since the day he had known
>about himself,
>his Father,
>and his mission?
>Shouldn't he turn
>the stones of this world
>into bread and gold
>to save himself
>alone?

Shouldn't he use his extraordinary possibilities
to realize the most fantastic one-man show
ever performed
with applause from all sides?
>Shouldn't he use his power
>to rule them all,
>with the crack of his whip,
>he had used in the temple,
>making them turn left, right,
>forward and backward?

Shouldn't he live
the life they were all living,
the only life-possibility
they knew?
>Would it be worth it
>to change it all?

He thought of the cross,
his death
and his blood,
the wounds
and the dirt.
>Would they understand?
>Would anyone ever understand?
>Would the new ever grow,

the seed he was going to sow
in the tomb
of this earth?
Philip and Andrew
must have been wondering
about his reaction.
Probably they did not understand it
at all.
Did he say *yes*
or did he say *no*?

But before he had finished
his answer,
his agony was over,
the decision taken,
the *yes* was said.
And a voice from heaven
sounded as the echo to that *yes*:
glory, glory,
alleluia.

Sentence was passed,
the prince of the world overthrown,
life would start
afresh.

20.

THE FIGHT HE FOUGHT

Mark 14:1–15, 47

First there was that jubilant crowd,
tearing branches from the trees,
throwing flowers in front of his feet,
waving banners and flags.
They were singing and shouting,
around that man
on his she-ass,
all their hopes seemed to be fulfilled.
  They thronged around
  the one
  who only did good
  and never did evil;
  around the one
  who took children in his arms,
  who consoled their mothers and their fathers,
  who helped those who were confused,
  who healed those who were sick,
  who loosened all kinds of bonds,
  who purified the temple
  and who gave an example,
  a model, and a new chance,
  a possibility to everyone.

Around him
the clouds broke,
the rain came down,
grace after grace,
blessing after blessing,
the dry land of their lives
opened up
and became green,
full of flowers, seeds,
plants, and animals,
life,
new life everywhere.
      Then there was that angry mob,
      the terrible way
      in which they took him,
      arrested him,
      betrayed him,
      and crucified him
      using the wood of the tree
      from which they had pulled the branches
      and the flowers
      to applaud him.
The passion story by Mark
is a shocking story
about him
caught up
in the struggle
between good and evil
that is ravaging our world
and ourselves
all the time.
      The stories of today,
      the story of that "*alleluia*"
      and the story of the "*crucify him*"
      are the stories of the world
      in which we live,
      hate, and love.
Judas kissed him
into his ordeal;

Peter betrayed him
after his oath to be faithful;
the Sanhedrin tried to stick to the law,
but the evidence accepted was conflicting;
Pilate condemned him,
saying: "Why, what harm has he done?";
the soldiers crucified him
admitting: "He is the Son of God."
> It was in them,
> it is in us,
> that he is glorified;
> it was in them,
> it is in us,
> that he was crucified;
> it was in them,
> it is in us,
> that he shouted:
> My God, my God,
> why have you forsaken me?;
> It was in them,
> it is in us,
> that he will rise.
Love and hate,
we don't take that struggle in us
seriously,
we don't take that struggle in others
seriously,
we don't take that struggle in the world
seriously.
> Some say:
> we are saved already
> and all is good;
> some say:
> all is bad,
> there is no hope;
> others say
> that all of us are hypocrites,
> speaking good
> and doing bad.

Not all is good,
not all is bad,
not all is hypocrisy:
the reality
is that fight between good and evil,
            between light and dark,
            between new and old;
a fight in which he participated,
he,
the Son of God,
and goodness
wins.

21.

LEAVING YOUR FEET
IN HIS HANDS

John 13: 1–15

They were sitting at table,
it was at the beginning of the meal,
Judas had made up his mind
to betray him.
Jesus looked at the clock,
his hour had come,
he came from his place at table,
he took his tunic off,
and his shirt too,
he was now in his underwear.
    He took a towel
    and a washbasin,
    he filled the basin
    with water
    and he started to wash their feet.
    When he came to Peter,
    he took the feet of Peter
    in his hands.
    Peter pulled them again
    out of his hands
    while saying:

never in all eternity
are you going to wash
my feet.
He said this
out of respect.
He told Jesus:
respect yourself,
don't do this,
don't humiliate yourself like this,
think where you come from,
consider who you are.

     It was the old temptation;
     again Peter said:
     escape from us,
     escape from the world,
     get to heaven.

Jesus took Peter's feet again
in his hands
and he said,
while looking at him:
if you don't let me wash your feet,
you will never be
with me.

     If I escape from you
     now,
     you will be lost forever;
     if I don't remain with you,
     where will you go?

And he washed Peter's feet,
and also the feet
of all the others.

     He sat again down with them
     at table.
     He took his bread,
     and he said to them:
     you see what I do,
     and he broke the bread,
     that is what I am going to do for you
     with myself.

They looked at him,
they got tears in their eyes,
though they did not understand.
> He was with them,
> he remained with them,
> though Peter had told him
> to go,
> because he himself had been scared
> when he had taken his feet
> in his hands.
He remained with them,
he remains with us,
and our feet should remain
in his hands
even if they are led
where we wouldn't like
to go:
his kingdom
to come.

22.

GOD'S GUARDED TOMB

John 18: 1–19:42

He had been arrested.
He had been caught.
He had refused to escape from their hands.
His face had been battered.
He had been standing before judges
who had made up their minds about him
long before they had ordered his arrest.
He had been hanging on the cross
for three full hours
in agony and pain,
and now he was dead.

    Nature shrunk away from this horror.
    An earth tremor was felt.
    The sanctuary of the temple
    was stripped of its sanctity:
    its covering curtain torn from top to bottom,
    naked,
    open to everybody.
    The sun disappeared in the middle of the day.
    It became dark,
    pitch dark.

He was dead,
the just one,
the one sent by God,
God,
dead in the middle
of his creation.
The birds went into hiding,
animals crouched together in their holes,
notwithstanding all the clouds
the rain refused to fall,
there was lightning but no thunder,
graves opened,
ghosts were seen.
God died in the middle of his handiwork,
he died in the hearts of the priests,
at the moment that they were condemning
an innocent one.
God died in the hearts of the crowd
that refused to accept
his unconditional goodness
in their own lives.
God died in Pilate
who said:
he has done no harm,
but go ahead,
scourge him,
kill him.
God died in Peter
who lied:
I,
I don't know that man,
who is he in any case?
and the cock crowed
in horror.
He hanging on the cross
had shouted
just before he died:
my God, my God,
why have you forsaken me?

and bending his head,
he sighed out
his last breath.
He was not the first one
who died like that,
there had been so very many before him,
just ones and prophets,
real prophets not thinking
about their own bread,
but about the bread of others.

      He would not be the last one
      to die like that,
      so many would follow him,
      so many are following him
      even at this very moment,
      standing before judges,
      tortured by interrogators
      in whom God is as dead
      as he was in that tomb,
      that totally new tomb in this world,
      the tomb of God.
Even his murderers could not believe
that they had succeeded.
They did not feel fine,
they did not feel safe.
How had this been possible?
He had not resisted at all.
He had kept quiet most of the time.
He had looked around himself
from the cross
in a way they did not like at all
and even that Roman officer had said
something about God
when he saw him die.

      They went to Pilate,
      to be sure that he would be kept
      in his grave.
      Seals were not sufficient,
      they had said,
      they wanted a guard.

Pilate agreed,
because that is what he wanted too,
a guard.
He was afraid
that the nightmare
that had visited his wife
the night before
would be his
for quite some time
to come.
And there they stood
in front of his tomb,
scared
that goodness
and godliness
might burst forth once more
from that tomb
into the garden,
into the world,
into the hearts of all.
They stood and
they watched
trembling with an ever-increasing
feeling
that it would be good
to be ready
to run.

23.

EARLY IN THE MORNING

Mark 16: 1-8

It was very early in the morning
when Mary of Magdala,
Mary the mother of James,
and Salome
hurried to the grave
in the light of the rising sun.
>They had been buying all the ingredients
>necessary for an embalmment.
>They were in a hurry,
>they had only one thing on their minds,
>to get to his body
>and to embalm it properly
>as soon as possible
>to preserve it
>as long as possible.
They had been in such a rush
that they seemed to have overlooked
some very practical points,
not only the weight of the heavy stone
in front of the tomb,
but also the official seals,

118

the military guards,
and things like that.
       When they arrived
       the soldiers were not there
       and the stone had been rolled away.
       Mark does not tell us
       how they reacted to that.
       They might have thought that others,
       maybe his own mother,
       had got there
       before them
       having the same idea
       of embalming him.
They went inside
and got the shock of their lives.
There were no others
but only someone in white
sitting at the right side
on the slab of rock
on which Jesus had been buried.
       When the young man
       saw their fear
       he said,
       raising his hand:
       Don't be afraid,
       you are looking for Jesus,
       aren't you?
       He is no longer here,
       he is risen,
       look there is the place
       where he was buried
           —they looked
           and the only thing they saw
           was the shroud
           folded up in a corner.
       They looked at him again:
       Go to his disciples,
       go to Peter,

tell them
that he left already for Galilee
to meet them
as he had told them
that he would do.
They did not listen anymore;
they ran from that tomb
as fast as they could
fleeing into the garden
out of their wits with fear
and because of that flight
they decided not to tell anyone
anything at all.
They were terrified
and yet they were not women
easily giving in to fear.
At least two of them
had braved the scorn of the crowd,
the priests, and the soldiers
while he was hanging on the cross
remaining there up to the moment
of his death.
They had remained to assist
in his improvised burial
without any fear overwhelming them.
But now they were suddenly
out of their minds,
reports Mark,
suggesting that they were running away
like frightened chickens.
What happened to them?
What made the difference?
His arrest had been a terrible shock,
but was it not something to be expected
as the normal course of events
in the world in which we live?
Is not every head stuck out
in favor of goodness and justice
threatened to be chopped off?

His death had been another shock
but again was it not something to be expected
after the beating he underwent
not to speak about his crucifixion?
His burial had been shocking too
in the dark of that evening
with so little time
and the sabbath so near.
>   All that
>   belonged to the life
>   and the death
>   they knew.
>   But this empty tomb
>   was something totally different.
>   It meant a total break
>   with what they had been accustomed
>   to.
They were frightened
not so much because of that empty tomb,
not even because of that risen life,
but because they felt,
because they knew
that this was going to change
the whole of their lives.
>   If he had risen from the dead
>   then his life would be,
>   from that rising onwards,
>   the model and the norm
>   for the life of all,
>   asked for
>   and guaranteed
>   by God.
They understood
that what had happened to him
would have to happen to them,
would have to happen to us.
And suddenly
in those first moments
of that realization,

their old lives
felt as empty as that tomb
and they ran and ran,
to be found by him,
to be filled with a life
that was new
to them.
Alleluia.

24.

HE GREETED THEM

John 20: 19–31

The gospel reading of this Sunday
is a very rich one.
It is about belief and unbelief,
it is about being sent
and about what to do in case
of failure and sin,
it is about his Spirit
in us.
>But let us today
>consider a seemingly more simple issue.
>Let us reflect
>upon something Jesus does
>three times
>in the gospel of today,
>twice during his first apparition
>and once during his second one.
>Three times he greets them:
>*"Peace be with you."*
>Three times,
>and they must have been very glad
>because of that.

123

Jesus had appeared that morning
to women
and not to them.
They had seen the empty tomb
but not
him.

They were not surprised.
Had they not betrayed him?
Had they not run away from him?
Had they not denied him?
They had come together
because of all the stories
and all the rumors.
One, Thomas, was even missing.
They did not know what to do.

Then, suddenly,
without anybody having seen him coming,
he stood in their midst.
They would have panicked,
they would have run to the doors and the windows
if he had not put out his hands
saying:
"Peace be with you,
peace be with you!"

That greeting meant
that he wished them well,
that greeting meant
that he was glad to see them,
that greeting meant
that he wished them life and happiness,
that greeting meant
that he enjoyed seeing them again.
All was well again.
That greeting was to them
like a real blessing,
and they relaxed,
and they started to talk together
all at the same time
excitedly.

He had greeted them,
he had greeted them!

We are so accustomed
to greeting each other,
to shaking hands
left, right, and center
that we might overlook
its significance.
But remember that time
that you were in company
and you met an old friend
or a colleague.
You stretched out your hand
to greet him,
and he did not greet you
and you did not know what to do
with your hand
dangling in the air,
and you felt
that he did not wish you well,
that he did not enjoy seeing you,
that he wished you dead,
and all the others saw it,
and you felt very embarrassed.
If greeting is a *blessing*,
not greeting is a *curse*.

Some weeks ago I met someone,
someone quite educated,
who had come to town
for the first time.
We were standing at the Main Campus.
I asked her:
do you like town?
She obviously did not know
what to answer.
I changed my question:
what strikes you most about town?
I thought she was going to say
the traffic, the high buildings,

or the variety of goods in the shops.
She did not answer immediately,
she looked around
and finally said:
"People don't greet each other
in town, it seems."
I looked around myself;
all kinds of people
were milling around us,
and it was true:
they did not greet
each other.
She continued:
"They speak to each other,
but they do not greet each other.
They do not seem to enjoy
each other's existence."
It is sometimes strange
how things coincide,
because when I browsed
in the library some days later
I found a book called
Antique Chinese Wisdom;
looking in that book
I found a proverb, or better a riddle.
It read:
"What is the best of these three:
teaching, a story, or a greeting?"
The answer was given too:
a greeting.
The answer was even explained:
a greeting is best
because without that greeting
each teaching,
each story,
will fall flat.
Jesus greeted them
three times,
and after that he said:

"As the Father sent me,
so I am sending you.
Peace be with you!"
In almost all his letters Paul asks
the Romans, the Corinthians, the Thessalonians,
and us
to greet each other.
Peter in his letters
does the same.

Greet each other,
bless each other,
be open to each other,
recognize the Spirit, his Spirit,
in yourself and in each other.
To greet is to bless.
To bless is to greet.
To greet means:
I am open to you.
To be greeted means
that someone wished you well,
that God is with you,
that God is with us.

It is after having greeted him
that Jesus said to Thomas:
put your finger here
and believe.
Was it that finger that did it
or was it his greeting?
I don't know,
but Thomas said:
My Lord and
my God.

25.

THE HELP HE GAVE

Luke 24: 35–48

Help is a good thing.
To help somebody in need
is a gospel obligation.
To help is also a dangerous thing.
    Like in so many countries,
    in this country too,
    help sometimes proves to be almost fatal.
    There are
    according to very reliable reports
    chickenhouses unfinished,
    cattledips started
    but never fully realized,
    because
    while the locals started to construct them,
    an expert from the government,
    or the representative of one or another
    overseas organization,
    or a passing tourist,
    promised
    help from outside.
    At the moment
    that the promise was made

people sat down
and started to wait
until the help came.
A professor here at the University
made a study
on self-reliance, *harambee*, and help from abroad.
He came to astounding conclusions:
if the help that is put in a project from outside
reaches 10 percent of the total investment
the local effort
stops.

This is true not only
in this country.
It is true in any country,
it is true in any assistance program,
it is true in any social welfare work.
It is true,
or at least a danger too,
in religious matters.
Jesus must have known this
very well!

He had saved them,
they said and they say,
and they looked and they look
at him
day and night.
He had saved them
they said and they say,
and they made and make pictures of him
with nice "blue" eyes
or eyes as brown
as the eyes of a gazelle.

He had saved them
they said and they say,
and they started to sing their songs
dancing together around him,
strumming their guitars
yodeling their "praise the Lord's,"
alleluia.

He had saved them
they said and they say,
and they sat down in the bliss
of the light
shining from his face
on them.
> He had saved them
> they said and they say,
> and it did not change their lives
> at all;
> they went on as ever before
> and the world remained
> as it was,
> except for him.
In fact it became worse,
because they forgot,
who they had been.
> I hope that you will not be scandalized
> to hear
> that some philosophers and sociologists say
> that for that reason
> the preaching of Jesus Christ
> in cultures that were self-reliant before
> can be a *disaster*.
> That it often emasculates
> the original strength and power.
> That it sometimes demoralizes
> a population
> because instead of relying on themselves
> and the morality and religiosity
> developed by themselves,
> they start to look at that person
> outside of themselves:
> Jesus Christ.
Those researchers hold
that the preaching of Jesus
is to a great extent
the cause of the corruption
all around us

in this continent
and in the world!
     It is for that reason too
     that someone whose name is often
     more a myth
     than anything else,
     Karl Marx,
     disliked and really hated
     religious people.
     He said of them
     that they were useless,
     that they were alienated
     from reality
     and from the world.
     He said of them
     that they were passive,
     a hindrance,
     a block on the legs
     of those who wanted
     to change the world.
Jesus must have known this danger
very well.
He did not have to foresee it;
he could see it
in their eyes,
in their faces,
in their way of looking
at him.
     When he showed his hands,
     they said to each other:
     "Look at *his* hands";
     when he showed them his feet,
     they said to each other:
     "Look at *his* feet";
     when they looked at his side,
     they said to each other:
     "Look at *his* side";
     when they touched his hands,
     they said to each other:

"Feel *these* hands";
when they touched his feet,
they said to each other:
"Feel *these* feet";
when they touched his side,
they said to each other:
"Gosh, how deep was *his* wound."
He saw it in their fear
that he might be only a ghost;
he saw it in their joy
that made them
—as the gospel literally wrote—
dumbfounded:
      chickens around the mother hen,
      children pressing around the lap
      of their mother.
And he tried,
and tried
and tried
every time he met them
to overcome that blockage
in them.
That is why he spoke,
even while being with them
about himself
in the past tense:
"while I *was* still with you."
That is why he appeared
and disappeared.
That is why
he tells them
at each apparition
in one way or another:
      "Now it is up to you,
      forgiveness is up to you,
      the changing of the world is up to you,
      the spreading of the word is up to you,
      the start of the kingdom is up to you,
      the charity, the justice, the peace, the unity,
      it is all up to you.

I will send the Holy Spirit
to you.''
''I am going,''
he had said long before,
while looking at them,
''How good will it be
when I leave you.
Because if I did not leave you,
you would never realize
your own spirit,
your own possibilities,
your own humanity,
your own divinity.''
The gospel reading today
reports:
he opened *their* eyes
and he told *them*
YOU are going to witness
from here in Jerusalem
all over the earth.
YOU!

26.

WE ARE POOR SHEPHERDS INDEED

John 10: 11–18

We had a day of retreat
in our community not long ago.
Many of you participated.
Someone gave an introduction,
to help us on the way.
He gave a kind of talk on prayer.
A kind of talk,
because it was a very strange talk.
It was as if the speaker were surprised
all the time
by what he was saying.
He had a Bible
and some books
and some papers.
He looked in those books,
he looked in those papers,
he looked at us,
and then he would say something
and then he would look at the sky
and at the trees
and again at us

and he would repeat what he had said
once more;
he would take up his Bible,
put it down again
and say what he said
a third time,
a fourth time.
It was as if he were
—while speaking to us—
discovering his own thoughts,
his own heart,
his own mind,
his own depth.
     Jesus
     might have been a bit like that
     while speaking to them
     that morning.
     He said:
     I am the shepherd;
     he repeated:
     I am the good shepherd.
     He said:
     I am willing to die for the sheep;
     he repeated:
     I am willing to die for them.
He too must have looked at the sky,
he too must have looked at them,
he too must have looked at himself
and he said again:
I am willing to give up my life,
I give it up of my own free will,
I have the right to give it up.
     He must have been surprised
     about himself,
     about what he heard himself say,
     about the vision opened,
     about all he suddenly understood
     in the clear light
     of the will of his Father.

The person I spoke about
in the beginning of this reflection
had a theme like that.
He read a psalm to us,
I forgot which one,
but he said
when you read such a psalm,
when you pray such a prayer,
you see
how God sees all at the same time,
that God overlooks our whole life,
that God does not look at today or tomorrow,
at this success or that failure,
at this frustration or that joy,
at this sin or that act of virtue:
God sees all,
God does not compartmentalize,
God does not say: now you are a failure,
God does not work digitally like a computer
in which continuously data about you are fed.
God is,
        —and again he looked at the sky,
        at us,
        and at himself—
God is a shepherd to us all,
God is a shepherd to life,
Jesus is a shepherd to life,
and we should be like him,
we should be like him . . .
        and he laid his papers down,
        and he took his Bible,
        and he looked at the sky,
        and he looked at us,
        and he looked at himself,
        and he laid his Bible down,
        and he took his papers up,
        and he repeated:
        we should be like him.

When Jesus says: I am the good shepherd
he is speaking about his care for human life.
When Jesus says: I am sending you, as I was sent,
he is speaking about our care for human life.
When he said: I am the good shepherd,
he meant to imply: and you should be good shepherds too.
    We had this week
    here in our community
    two talks,
    two introductions.
    One was about human rights as implemented
    in Kenya,
    the other one was about the care for the environment
    in Kenya.
    Both talks were in fact
    about being good shepherds
    to life.
Dr. Gutto spoke about the right to life
as guaranteed by the Kenyan constitution to all;
he explained that that is the reason
that Kenyan law considers
voluntary abortion a crime:
we should be good shepherds to life.
He added, however,
that no one,
neither pope nor bishop,
ever seems to bother
about all those spontaneous abortions
that take place
because the women in question are undernourished,
starving or sick,
without any help,
while others have much too much:
we are no good shepherds at all!
    Francis Lelo explained
    how we ruin our environment
    by deforestation,
    by throwing our dirt all over,

by polluting the rivers and lakes;
we are poor shepherds indeed.
He said: I am the good shepherd,
I take care.
He added:
I am sending you,
as I was sent,
good shepherds
indeed?

27.

SOWING A SEED

John 15: 1–8

Jesus compares himself
and us together with him
to a vine,
to a plant,
to a tree.
> He tells us
> that the life he brought to this world
> is like the life of a plant.
> He had spoken earlier
> about the life he brought
> as a seed
> that would grow into a plant,
> as a seed
> that would grow into a tree
> so high
> that all would be able to build a nest
> in its crown.
That sounds very nice,
it sounds very rustic,
it sounds very rural,
but it sounds also slow,
very, very slow.

139

And I think that it is that slowness
that can irritate us,
and that does irritate us
so mightily.
> We are modern people,
> we can do things,
> we can work miracles,
> we build a big house in a very short time,
> we drive from Mombasa to Busia
> in less than a day,
> we can fly it in a couple of hours
> and we have no patience left
> to sit down
> and see the trees and the plants and the flowers
> grow.
> Who has the time for that?
> Who ever saw a tree grow?
And yet we all know
that the wood we use
to build our houses
came from plants that grew
very, very slowly.
We all know
that the oil we use
to rush or to fly
from here to there
came from minuscule plants
that needed millions and millions of years
to amass themselves
to be ready for us.
> Did you ever hear that story
> about a carpenter
> living in a country
> that is not so far off any more
> where there was only one forest?
> Every time he needed wood
> for his coffee tables
> and his chairs,
> for his doors and his windowframes,

for his floors and his roofs
he went to the forester,
until the day the last tree
was cut
and the forester told him to wait
until new trees had grown up,
and that carpenter was very amazed
that he had to wait for years and years
before he finally got them.
And he started to work
with so much more care
and even respect.
Jesus compares the growth
he brought,
the new life he introduced:
the kingdom of God,
the kingdom of God,
the kingdom of God
with that growth,
with that very slow growth.

He did not do that once,
he did it
over and over again:
the kingdom of God is like a man
who sowed seeds;
the kingdom of God is like a man
who took a mustardseed
and sowed it in his field.
You know
that there is an everlasting discussion
raging already for more than a century
whether we were created
at once,
in one go,
or whether we were created
through a very slow growth
called evolution.
Practically every week
you can find *letters to the editor*

about this issue
in the local press.
>Nobody seems to be sure
>how things, how we developed.
>But we got the information
>about the life Jesus brought
>into this world:
>it will grow,
>it will grow,
>it is growing all around us,
>even in ourselves
>if we remain connected
>to him.

There is an objection
we can make.
Did not his disciples
in those early days
of the Acts of the Apostles
realize it at once?
Don't we read in those Acts:
>"The whole group of believers was united,
>heart and soul,
>no one claimed for his own use anything he had,
>everything they owned was held in common.
>None of their members was ever in want,
>as all those who owned land or houses
>would sell them
>and bring the money from them
>to present it to the apostles;
>it was then distributed to any members
>who might be in need."

That is true,
it is the model.
It did, however, not remain like that
as we all know.
It was possible
in their time,
in their days
because they believed
that the end of the world,

that the final return of Jesus
was only a question
of a year or so.
>Wouldn't you be doing the same
>if you knew
>that Jesus would come very soon,
>maybe tomorrow
>or the day after that?
We often blame the church,
we often blame ourselves
that all is corrupt,
that nothing goes,
that the ideal is never reached.
>We don't see the growth
>of the *tree of life*
>he planted in this world.
>But who ever saw
>a tree
>actually grow?
Growing it did
as was said in the first reading today:
>"The churches throughout Judea, Galilee, and Samaria
>were now left in peace,
>building themselves up,
>living in the fear of the Lord,
>filled with the consolation of the Holy Spirit,"
>pushing on,
>growing.
Sometimes
I am very depressed.
Things do not seem to advance.
You wonder whether the word and the seed
did not get lost.
Do you know what I do
when I feel like that?
>I sow a seed,
>and I watch it grow,
>every morning and every evening.
>I never see the growth
>and it grows,

getting leaves and branches,
buds and flowers,
seeds and fruits
sometimes
a hundredfold.
We should keep pushing on,
we should remain attached,
we should let his life grow in us,
together with him
during the day and during the night
and in the end
the smallest of seeds
will be the biggest of all:
a tree
in the shadow of which
all evil, stupidity,
and sin
will have withered
long ago.

28.

CAN LOVE BE COMMANDED?

John 14: 15–21

It is the story you know.
It is a story told so very often.
It is a story we know so very well
that sometimes we overlook its force.
  She said:
  I was a child in a very large family.
  I was in the middle somewhere.
  I am sure that my father and my mother loved me,
  and so did my brothers and sisters;
  we were not rich,
  we were hardly surviving
  and the school fees for me and the others
  were a real burden to my parents.
  My father worked the whole day,
  so did my mother.
  There was not very much time left
  to talk with each other.
  Everyone was so busy.
  I had accepted myself,
  the others had accepted me,
  but I thought myself rather plain
  and very common,
  nothing special.

145

Then I met him.
He looked at me.
I saw him looking,
I wondered what he saw.
And then he said to me:
you are very pretty;
and he said to me:
you are beautiful;
and he said to me:
may I be your friend;
and he said to me:
you are my all and everything;
and he said to me:
I am thinking all the time of you.
My whole life,
my whole life
changed completely.
I looked at myself with other eyes
when standing in front of the mirror.
I looked with other eyes
at everything around me:
the sun and the moon,
the flowers and the birds,
the water and the air:
I was loved,
I was loved
and I loved;
I could have danced
all day
and all night.
You know also
the reverse of that story,
that feeling that nobody loves you.
How often did I not hear people say
with tears in their eyes,
with fists hopelessly clenched:
nobody loves me,
nobody loves me.
It is only in the context
of that love,

the warp and the woof
of all our novels and plays and films,
the substance of all our lives,
that we can understand
the reading of today
in which Jesus says:
"I love you,
you are my friends,
I am willing to give my life for you,
don't think that it is only you who decided to love me,
but I love you,
because *I* love *you*.
He went further
by commanding us
to love him
and to love each other.
This is my commandment
that you love each other.

It is that word "commandment"
that sounds strange
when speaking about love.
Can love be commanded?
Can I tell you:
you have to love me?
Can you tell another:
you have to love me?
That is the reason why some translate
that word commandment by "prescription."
The type of prescription
you find in a cooking book,
the kind of prescription
you find on the piece of paper
a doctor gives you,
indicating the type of medicine
you have to use
in order to become healthy.

You cannot cook *chicken and rice*
without rice.
you cannot cook *sorbotel**
without pork;

you cannot produce
ugali na nyama†
without a piece of meat.
That meat is prescribed,
it is a condition,
it is a commandment.
It is in that way
that Jesus says:
you cannot have human life
without love.
You cannot.
The reason being
that we exist
because we are loved
and it is only in that line,
in the line of that power
that we live,
that we can live,
see and can see,
taste and can taste,
smell and can smell,
touch and can touch.
    Without that divine ingredient
    human life
    is hell.

*Sorbotel: a Goan pork dish.
†*Ugali na nyama*: maisemeal and meat.

29.

IN AND OUT

Mark 16: 15–20

The ascension of the Lord
remains one of the least understood events
in *our* lives.
>It was only a few days ago
>that I was asked to give a talk
>to a few hundred high-school students.
>They had given me as a title:
>*"Life after death, idea or reality."*
>When the talk was over,
>there was, of course, question-time.
>The first question asked
>was not a question
>but a critical remark,
>or better a lament.
>A student said
>that he thought it a scandal
>that preachers were always preaching
>to look up to heaven,
>especially when their listeners
>are poor
>and sick
>and frustrated.

When he had made his remark
almost all of those present
shouted "point!"
and then started to clap their hands.
If it is true what that student said
—and it must be true
otherwise the others would not have applauded—
then ascension,
and what happened at the ascension of the Lord
was never preached
by those preachers.
Because if you read the ascension-story of today
then you can see and hear
that that is exactly
what Christians are NOT supposed to do.

The two angels in the story
say: NO,
to the followers of Jesus:
NO,
don't remain standing there,
gazing up to heaven.
Your task is to go to Jerusalem
and to wait for the promised Spirit
who will lead you
with the gospel
to the ends of the earth.

They went to Jerusalem,
they went to the upper-room
to wait,
and while they were waiting,
now without him,
they must have become
more and more aware of him,
of what he meant to them,
about the difference he made
in their lives.

While he had been with them,
they had taken him for granted
just as a child takes his mother for granted

until something happens to the mother
and suddenly
there is no food and no warmth,
no shelter and no security.
Just as we take so many things
for granted
until they fall away.
And experiencing him
in that new way
they must have been coming
closer and closer
together.
For the first time
they themselves
formed his community
among each other
with the doors closed
and the windows shuttered,
with the doorbell turned off
and no outsiders allowed.
        And heaven,
        which they were not allowed
        to look up to,
        seemed to be realized
        in their midst:
                with their bread broken
                and their wine shared,
                with prayers together
                and peace assured.
That was good
and they felt fine;
that was great
and they felt good;
that is why they were sent
to Jerusalem,
to be together,
but it was not the end:
there were those ends of the earth
waiting for them.

Again a misunderstanding threatened to grow,
as it threatens so often to develop amongst us,
in our communities and our families.
Again they were gazing,
so to speak,
in heaven,
but now as realized in their togetherness,
and the world around them
remained unchanged,
though they prayed very much,
though they formed an excellent community
and kept peace very well.
>It was as if his kingdom,
>his power and its force,
>were restricted to their table,
>to their kitchen,
>their possessions,
>and their lives,
>domesticated
>beyond recognition.
They had not forgotten
that they had to wait,
which meant
that not all
had been fulfilled,
that not all
had been revealed,
and they waited
up to the moment
that his Spirit
scattered them
all over the world
as far as feet and beast and ship
could carry them.
>They were brought
>together
>to receive his Spirit
>and they were sent out
>as witnesses to that.

It is in that tension
of *in*
and *out*
that we should live
and work,
and if we don't do that
heaven will remain
a far-off reality,
looked at
from a distance
only.

30.

THEY ALL SPOKE
OF THE GREAT THINGS
GOD HAD DONE

John 20: 19–23

It is Pentecost,
the fiftieth day after Easter,
the day of the Holy Spirit.
The readings
abound in their descriptions
of that Spirit:
> There is the powerful wind,
> the noise that filled the whole house;
> there is that bundle of tongues of fire
> that separated itself
> over them;
> there was the gift of languages
> and the thousands believing
> in the streets.
But then there is that contrasting picture
of him standing among them
the evening of that same day,
Easter day,

with the doors closed,
saying:
Peace be with you,
as the Father sent me
so I am sending you.
Breathing,
just breathing,
not even blowing,
breathing over them saying:
receive the Holy Spirit,
for those whose sins you forgive
they will be forgiven.
     And finally there is Paul
     speaking about the influence
     of the Holy Spirit
     in our lives:
     no one can say
     Jesus is the Lord
     except in that Spirit;
     all the services we render to each other,
     all the works we work,
     all the gifts and talents we use,
     it is all from the same Spirit.
The Jerusalem wind and fire
is over.
Jesus does not appear any more.
The Spirit remained,
as Paul wrote.
in the humdrum
of our daily lives,
hidden and most times
unnoticed by us.
     Being not noticed
     does not mean
     not being there!
Some weeks ago
we had here in our community
three sessions
on how to pray.

In order to pray
one has first to concentrate,
to become quiet
and peaceful.
Three methods were given
for that concentration,
and all three methods came in a way
to the same:
to get aware
of experiences we have
without noticing them.

> There is the breathing
> that goes on in us all the time.
> So get aware of that breathing,
> sit down very easily,
> close your eyes
> and watch your breath;
> is it very fast?
> slow it down,
> is it superficial?
> make it deep,
> control it,
> get aware.

There is the hearing
that goes on in us all the time.
So get aware of that hearing,
sit down very easily,
close your eyes
and listen to every noise you hear,
let those noises penetrate you
deeply and freely,
get aware.

> There are the bodily sensations
> you are feeling all the time.
> So get aware of those feelings,
> close your eyes,
> sit down very easily,
> feel the touch of your clothes on your shoulders,
> feel the touch of your clothes on your back,

feel your back touching the chair,
feel the touch of your hands resting on each other,
get aware
and peace will set in.
Without some concentration,
the presence of the Holy Spirit,
the fruits of Pentecost,
will remain as unnoticed to us
as our breathing,
   our hearing,
   our bodily sensations.
      Some days ago I asked
      some schoolchildren
      to tell me about the Holy Spirit.
      They told me
      about the fire,
      about the storm,
      about Peter on the balcony,
      about the languages,
      about the baptisms in the street;
      when I asked them:
      did you ever notice
      the work of the Holy Spirit
      in yourselves
      and in the others around you,
      no one knew what to answer;
      they looked at me
      with large querying eyes.
      I changed the question
      and asked them:
      did you ever do anything
      really good?
      And again they had
      no answer.
      I asked:
      did your parents,
      your father and your mother,
      ever do anything
      really good?

Again there was
no answer.
So I said:
sit down comfortably,
close your eyes
and ask yourself
what good did I do?
They did sit down
as easily as they could,
they did close their eyes
and then
slowly, slowly
the answers came:
one had saved a small child
out of a river;
one had forgiven
her sister;
one said:
my mother takes care
of me;
another said:
my father helped
a poor man,
and
slowly, slowly
they started to become aware
of the goodness, the love, the care
in their daily lives:
the work of Holy Spirit.

Today is Pentecost;
the wind blew over,
though it blows sometimes still among us,
thank God;
the fire extinguished,
though it sometimes still heats our hearts,
thank God;
the gift of languages disappeared,
though some of us still speak in tongues
now and then,
thank God;

Jesus even left us
leaving his breath
in us,
and it is with that breath
that we live;
a breath we often do not notice,
what a pity;
a breath we don't often speak about,
what a shame;
but a breath that is in us!
So close your eyes,
sit down quietly
and get aware of his work in you.
If you do that today
this Pentecost
will bring you
nearer to him
and
to yourself.

31.

HEY, YOU UP THERE!

Matthew 28: 16–20

We are accustomed
to the word
God.
You use it,
I use it,
everyone uses it:
people who believe in God
and people who say
that they do not believe in God.
    Everyone who hears
    about an accident,
    about a sudden death,
    about a disaster,
    says almost spontaneously:
    my God,
    as if to indicate
    that a foundation
    has been rocked;
    as if to indicate
    that the order
    slipped away
    and should be restored
    by that final instance.

We take the word God
so often in our mouths
that we hardly ever
think about the meaning of that word,
if ever.
    To ask why do we call
    God God,
    seems to be as meaningless
    as to ask
    why do we call
    a table a table;
    why don't we call
    a table a chair.
I heard once a lecturer
who taught that the word God
was a word like table,
a mere conventional sound,
as such totally meaningless,
and to illustrate this
he added
that we could as well
have called God, dog
and dog, God.
    That is not correct.
    There is more to the word God
    than there is to the word table.
    The word God means something.
    It is not a mere sound,
    a conventional sign.
    The germanic word God
    means:
        "the one we call,"
        "the one we invoke,"
        "the one called,"
        "the one invoked,"
        the one we pray to.
    When using the name God
    we are showing
    that we are really at a loss.

The use of the word God
indicates
that we don't really
know
the name
of the one
we are calling to.
When we pray to him
we can't use his name.
That name God means
"Hey, you over there
in heaven,"
and nothing more.
You all know
how horrible it is
when you don't know
the name of a person,
of someone
you urgently need.
      You are in danger,
      your foot is trapped
      in a hole;
      you feel that a river
      is carrying you
      away;
      you feel
      that you are going to faint
      and there far, far away,
      but just within shouting distance
      is that other one
      you see;
      he is very busy,
      weeding his field:
      you shout
      and shout,
      but he does not look up
      from his work
      in the field
      between his maize-stalks,

and you say,
and you think,
and you know:
if only I knew his name,
then he would listen,
because now you can only shout:
"Hey, you,
you over there!"
and he does not look up
at all.
If only you knew his name,
if only you were able to shout:
"Hey, you, Kimani,
Kimani, help, help!"
You don't know his name,
you can't personalize your call
and that is why
you cannot reach him,
you cannot touch him,
he remains deaf
to your call.
That day
they had a date
with Jesus,
an appointment
on a mountaintop in Galilee.
On a mountaintop
you are symbolically
as near to God
—whom humanity invoked
almost always
as the one above us—
as possible.
That is why the people
here in East Africa
localized God
on the top of Mount Kenya,
on the top of Mount Elgon,
on the top of Mount Meru.

There on top of that mountain
he spoke
and he gave the names
of the one
up to then always
invoked by us
with the helpless:
"Hey, you up there,
in heaven!"
He called God
                    Father,
He called God
                    Son,
he called God
                    Spirit.
He called God
our source and our beginning;
he called God
the one with us now: Emmanuel;
he called God
the one who will be with us
for all the time to come
with that very slow growth.
There is an objection
we can make.
Did not his disciples
in those early days
of *the acts of the apostles*
realize it at once?
Don't we read in those *acts*:
        Three names,
        three persons,
        one God.
Jesus did not only
give us God's names;
he indicated at the same time
our relationship
to the one
we had only been able
to call God:

"Hey, you up there!"
till that moment,
though we had invented
—but in an unauthenticated way—
very many names.
He said:
      I have the authority,
      I know,
      I am allowed to reveal
      them: Father,
            Son,
            Spirit.
Let us live
like that,
let us pray
that humanity
may live
those names:
      in the name of the Father,
      and the Son,
      and the Holy Spirit.
      Amen.
      Let it be,
      let it be.

32.

THE TASK LEFT TO US

Mark 14: 12-16, 22-26

It might seem strange
that we celebrate Corpus Christi,
the feast of the body and blood of Jesus Christ,
at this point
of the liturgical year
after Pentecost,
Ascension,
and Trinity Sunday.
    Would it not have been better
    to celebrate it on Maundy Thursday
    on the day that Jesus
    —for the first time in that way—
    took his bread,
    shared his wine,
    and said:
        This is my body,
        this is my blood,
        do this to commemorate me.
Strange maybe
but full of meaning
if you come to meditate upon it.

Full of meaning
after all those more or less
"spiritualizing" feasts and commemorations.
Full of significance
in a period
where the Spirit who came to us
is so often misunderstood
and used as a reason
to get out of the life
we are living
or should be living.
With that bread in our hands
with that wine flowing through our system
we are facing the task
he left us
in an astonishingly concrete way.
He took the bread
and while breaking and sharing it
he said:
This bread,
this breaking,
this sharing
is my body.
He took his wine
and while handing it on and drinking it
he said:
This wine,
this drinking,
this sharing
is my blood.
All this was not only a rite,
all this was not only a touching gesture
to be repeated and repeated all over the world
in all the time to come;
all this left us
with a mission.
The mission of building his body,
by sharing our bread;

the mission of letting our wine
flow through all humanity.
A task
we can not fulfill
on our own.
A task
depending on our relations
with the Father
and the Son
and the Spirit.
A task that will be fulfilled
slowly
by our human decisions
in the light of our
faith
in him.
> What happened to his bread
> that night,
> what happened to his wine
> that evening
> should happen
> to the whole of humanity,
> to the whole of the world.
A French mystic
in our days,
Pierre Teilhard de Chardin,
saw this once
very clearly
while adoring
the Blessed Sacrament.
> He saw
> —in a vision—
> how suddenly the host
> he was looking at
> started to grow, to grow, to grow,
> until it contained
> all the world,
> interconnecting
> the whole of humanity.

And suddenly he understood,
    suddenly he *saw*.
This change-over
will not come
by some magical hocus-pocus.
That change-over
can come only
as the growth of his body
as the increase of his blood
through words spoken
and deeds done
       in the light of what he started
       that evening,
       the day before his death
       and some days before
       his resurrection.

33.

WITH HIS HEAD
ON A PILLOW

Mark 4: 35–41

That evening
they had set out
at his word.
It was he who had said:
"Let us cross over to the other side."
The other side
always promises
to be better
than this side.
     They had taken him on board
     notwithstanding the darkness of the sky,
     the darkness of the clouds
     and the direction of the wind,
     coming from the wrong corner,
     forecasting
     disaster.
Their experience told them
that it would be wiser
not to venture on the lake,
but after all
they were going with him,

with him
whom angels and devils
seemed to obey.
 Even when the storm
 broke loose,
 as they had expected,
 they were not alarmed
 as yet.
They pointed at him
over there in the stern of the boat
with his head peacefully
on a pillow,
a cushion
one of his admirers
had made for him.
 It was only when the water
 started to fill their boat
 with so much might and power
 that they were threatened
 to be swamped,
 that they woke him up
 and shouted:
 "Master, don't you care,
 we are going down?"
He woke up.
He looked around himself.
He stood up
leaving his pillow behind,
he raised his hand
and he ordered the wind,
calming the sea,
and all was quiet again.
Then he looked at them
and said:
"Why were you so afraid?
How is it
that you have no faith?"
 Their fear turned
 into awe,

that kind of reverential fear,
and they said to each other:
"How can this be,
how can this be?"
And they took their oars
—because he had not left them
a gust of wind any more—
and they rowed the boat
for the rest of the way
to that other side,
while he again
had laid his head
on that pillow,
made for him.
That awe
never left their lives
anymore
as long as they were
accompanying him.
Every step he made
seemed to be so new;
every word he spoke
made such a difference,
that they felt
their old securities
fall away
again and again.
The old situation
crumbled
under their eyes.
It was as if he said
all the time:
"Let us go away from here,
let us go to the other side!"
And he seemed to be so confident
about the possibility of that final outcome
that he simply put his head
on that pillow,
made for him.

34.

WHAT ABOUT THE POWER IN US?

Mark 5: 21-24, 35-43

Two stories in the gospel of today.
The story about that lady
who had been bleeding for over twelve years,
who had spent all her money on doctors,
but in vain:
she was getting worse and worse
every day
and her money had been finished
by the doctors around.
> The story about that girl of about twelve,
> who according to the people around her,
> her uncles and her aunts,
> her brothers and her sisters,
> her father and her mother,
> was dead,
> though Jesus said,
> that she was not dead
> but only asleep.
When Jesus said this
they laughed at him

and they continued
to prepare the funeral of the girl
they thought to be dead.
    I don't think
    that Jesus told a lie
    when he said that she was still alive.
    I think that he told the truth,
    the girl was not dead.
    It is true that she could not move,
    it is true that she could not speak,
    it is true that she hardly breathed
    but she must have heard
    all that was said around her.
    Don't we all know stories
    about people who seemed to be unconscious,
    but who told afterwards
    that they heard everything that was said
    around them,
    though they could not move
    and not speak
    and not answer?
You can imagine the horror
of that girl,
not able to move,
not able to speak,
when she heard about
digging a grave for her,
when she heard how
people were sent out
to buy a blanket
to bury her in.
She would have liked to shout:
stop it,
I am not dead!
    until Jesus came in
    who saved her
    from being buried alive!
The story about the lady with her bleeding
is not so very different.

She too was a dead living person.
Around her too people said
that she was non-existing,
that she was dead.
A lady with a sickness like hers
was cursed by the people among whom she lived.
She was not allowed to touch anyone,
and if anyone touched her
he was unclean,
he had to isolate himself
for eight days.
She was dead among the living.
       That is why the story tells
       that she came from the back;
       she could not come from the front,
       she would have been chased away
       as if she were a ghost,
       an evil spirit
       one not belonging to this world.
She touched Jesus,
nevertheless,
and while touching him
a power went out of him into her
and she was healed,
brought to full life.
       Brothers and sisters,
       aren't we too surrounded
       by those two;
       aren't we too
       surrounded by living people
       who seem to be dead?
The old people
left behind by their children
scraping their way through life
as spirits before their death.
       The poor people
       who in total destitution
       see their children die
       before their eyes.

The young people
without any future
and any chance among us.
>The sick and ill people
>who have no hope to heal
>and who, forgotten by all,
>are withering away
>for years and years.
People in prison
cut off
from all public and real human
life.
>In the gospel of today
>Jesus approaches this group of people
>in his world
>in our world.
>He does it twice
>and in both cases
>there is a power
>that goes out from him;
>in both cases
>he brings those living-dead
>those dead-living
>out of their torpor
>into the fullness of life;
>in both cases people jump up
>and start to live,
>>to dance,
>>to participate.
We carry his name,
we have his Spirit
he said of us
that we would do even greater things than he did
among those surrounding us,
among those who seem to be dead
though they are alive.
>Don't you know any of them
>in your family,
>among your acquaintances,
>among your neighbors?

It might be your old father,
it might be your old mother,
it might be your child,
might it be the one
your family kicked out?
Where are the followers of Jesus Christ,
the ones carrying his name,
who are willing to stretch out their hands
and to raise to life?
Where are those among you
so full of his Spirit
that they are conscious
of the power,
the life-giving power
that can flow out of them?

35.

AT HOME

Mark 6: 1-6

He finally returned
home.
They had been waiting for him;
he had not been back since he had gone to
John the Baptist.
Many of them
had gone to John,
they had listened to his message,
they had been willing to convert,
they had been kneeling in the water
in front of John,
they had felt the water
flow over their heads.
They had hoped very much
that they would change,
  but as so often
  in such cases
  not too much had really happened
  to them.
  Once back in their families,
  at home,

in their farms and their shops,
their enthusiasm had got lost;
all went on
as before.
He had not come back,
strange things had happened to him
during his baptism:
heaven had opened,
a voice had been heard
and he had disappeared
in the desert.
And after that
the strange stories about him
had never stopped.

John had ended his baptizing
because of him,
it was rumored.
He had changed a lot of water
into wine,
it was said.
He chased away evil spirits
and he healed the sick,
the story went.

They had been waiting for him,
and finally he had come.
They all went to the synagogue
that day
sure that he would be there.

He was.
And he sat down with them,
he stood up with them,
it was as if he had never been away.
Then
when someone was asked to do the reading
from the holy book,
he stood up again,
now alone;
he took the book
and he read to them
from the prophet Isaiah

about the change to come,
about the change
they had been hoping for.
They were amazed
at what he said
about prisoners who would be freed,
about broken hearts that would be healed,
about blind ones who would see,
about exploited and alienated ones
who would be delivered.

They listened more carefully,
and when they started
to understand
they first got upset
and then
very, very angry.
Because he seemed to be speaking
about them:

they were the alienated ones,
they were the blind ones,
they were the broken-hearted ones,
they were the prisoners,
they would have to change.
Who was he
that he dared to say
all that?

They stood up,
they pushed him out,
they took stones,
to get him down,
to cut him loose,
to put him out,
to do away with him,
but he walked through them,
facing them all,
unharmed.
Today
we hear him read
those same words
to us.

Those words
about broken hearts,
those words
about those imprisoned,
those words
about the blind,
those words
about the alienated ones;
     and all is well received
     as long as we can apply
     all those words
       —his judgment *on us*—
     to others,
     to those outside,
     to those responsible,
     to those high-up,
     to those far-away:
but isn't he speaking to us,
isn't he speaking to you and to me,
wasn't he speaking
to the ones related to him,
the ones of his own home,
the ones of his own family?
     We have invented so many ways
     to escape from his words,
     to do away with them,
     as they did away with him
     in Nazareth
     that day.
     We escape
     by painting sinners
     so dark
     and so evil
     that we are not like them;
     by painting the saints
     so soft
     and so sweet
     that we are in no way
     able to be like them
     either.

That is why he might say
also of us
that we have no faith in him,
and that he would not be able
to work through us
the miracles
our world
so very badly need
these days.

36.

HE SENT THEM OUT

Mark 6: 7–13

Something is changing in the church;
it is a change that is affecting all regions in the world;
it is not even necessary to quote statistics
to prove the existence of that change.
Everyone knows about it,
you can see it very easily.
> For some time
> the church has been accustomed
> to priests and to sisters and to brothers,
> plenty of them.
> They were well taken care of,
> they were in general not too badly off,
> they had a security,
> others, poorer people, could only dream of.
> Each village had its own priest,
> each village had its own sisters.
> Young women and men
> went to seminaries and scholasticates
> to be trained
> in an educational network
> that spanned the whole of the world
> and that no multinational would ever be able
> to match.

Now it suddenly is
as if all this came to
a complete standstill.
In fact it was only a situation
that existed in the West;
it never really worked
in other parts of the world
because of lack of personnel.
> The number of priests
> is going down,
> their average age is going up,
> and if no miracle happens
> a priest will be very soon
> as rare as a cardinal.
> The story of the gospel of today
> cannot be repeated anymore;
> there is nobody to be sent,
> though the call
> to preach a change,
> to preach repentance,
> to chase away evil spirits
> and to anoint and heal the sick
> seems to be more asked for
> than ever before.
Some people say
it is the fault of the church leadership:
why doesn't the Pope change his attitude
as regards obligatory celibacy for priests,
why does he restrict the priesthood to men only,
why do they give future priests a training that is
much more academic than pastoral,
and so on.
> As long as we are talking like that
> we might be overlooking another development
> that is taking place
> in that very same church
> we are members of.
Because of the growing lack
of the older, formal staff,
others are taking over.

We all know stories about
the small Christian communities
as they are called over here
in East Africa.
Those small Christian communities,
where so many of the tasks
of preaching and teaching,
of chasing devils and healing
are taken up
by the members themselves.
>We all must have heard
>about the basic Christian communities
>in South America;
>how men and women
>are organizing themselves
>in grassroots parish communities
>all over Europe.
>We all can very easily witness
>and read in practically any paper
>we see how those communities
>are insisting on change
>as regards the ownership of land and energy,
>as regards the money spent on armament,
>as regards health care,
>as regards the treatment of prisoners,
>and so on.
>They are members of no-nuke movements,
>they sympathize with *Amnesty International*,
>they fight against capital punishment,
>they struggle in favor of justice,
>they combat racism, tribalism,
>and genocide.
They are teaching and preaching
change and repentance,
they are actively chasing away evil and the devil,
they are anointing and healing.
>Although I told you in the beginning
>of this refleciton
>that there is no need to give
>any statistics,

let me give you one,
one only.
Did you know
that according to research
done in the United States of America
during *the year of the woman*,
not so long ago,
it was shown
that 25 percent of all Catholic women in the States
were involved in one or another church activity,
and that 95 percent of those 25 percent
were lay-women.
A very high number
you might think,
and that only in more or less formal
church activities,
others might observe.
But didn't Jesus
send out
ALL his disciples,
the 100 percent of them,
to teach,
to chase,
to heal?
What about you,
do you know yourself to be sent,
do you feel yourself to be sent,
into the world,
to get it changed and repenting,
purified and exorcised,
anointed and healed?

37.

HIS COMPASSION

Mark 6: 30–34

The gospel text of this Sunday
is very short,
not even 130 words,
and yet
in that very short text
Mark, the author,
mentions
Jesus' compassion
twice,
or in a way
even *thrice*.
>First he took pity
>on his disciples.
>They were coming back
>from their first trip.
>They had been preaching,
>they had been teaching,
>they had been chasing away evil spirits,
>they had been healing.
>Power had gone out of them
>all the time,

187

a power
they never had expected
in themselves.
They were very excited about it,
they had told each other and him
story after story.
The world was going to change
they were sure,
but it had cost them a lot,
and they dropped their sandals,
and they brushed their hair,
and they massaged their legs
and their arms,
and while they were giving each other
their reports
they were interrupted all the time
by dozens and dozens
who wanted to see them,
who wanted to be touched,
who wanted to draw their attention
to their sick children:
        they did not even have time
        for a bite,
        they did not even have a second
        for a drink,
        they were eaten alive
        by all those others.
He took *pity* on them
and he said:
let's get out of here,
you need a rest,
you need some time for yourselves
alone,
        and he organized a boat
        and a skipper
        and off they went.
They left
the others,
the dozens, the scores,

the hundreds and the thousands
behind.
It was so obvious,
however,
where they were going
that the crowd started
first to walk
and then to run
so that they were all there
when they arrived,
waiting again,
hoping again
to be touched.
> He took *pity* on them,
> sent his disciples off
> to have their rest,
> their drink and their meal,
> and he began to attend
> to that crowd
> himself.
We might think of that *compassion* of his
as something
that is not so very important
in the total richness
of his life.
It is a sentiment, however,
that is so often mentioned
as the *moving force*
in his work
that we have to be careful
about underrating it
in his personality set-up.
It was so much the force
that moved him
in his life
that it is not exaggerated to say
that he came in this world
because of his *pity*,
because of his compassion.

Every one of us knows
what Jesus must have felt
when he experienced
compassion.
Every one of us
has felt *pity*
from time to time,
    when seeing the smashed-up victim
    of a road accident;
    when hearing about an old father or mother
    left behind;
    when looking at the photo
    of some robbers shot down;
    when hearing about arrests and disappearances,
    when smelling the odor
    of unwashed children,
    stinking as the content of the dustbins
    they have been eating from.
We know of *pity*.
we feel *pity*,
but that does not mean
that we understand really
where that *pity* comes from
or what *pity's* significance
is.

    Once
    a mystic in Wales
    more than 300 years ago,
    Henry Vaughan, wrote this:
    "Charity is a relic from paradise
    and *pity* is a strange argument
    that we are all descended
    from one man."
It sounds rather mysterious
and very mystical
but he was right:
our compassion for others
derives from the fact
that we are one:

we all participate
in the same, human God-given life;
though many
we are one,
we form one communion
or at least:
we should.
And that is what we *know*,
and that is what we *feel*
when we see another one
smashed-up,
hungry,
thirsty,
frustrated,
or miserable.

There is something new
going round
in our world
these days.
More and more congregations and societies
of brothers and sisters,
more and more communities
of lay-people and priests
are becoming aware
of the necessity
to do something
about justice and peace.
This cannot be due
but to the fact
that our *pity* is growing;
due to a development
by which we feel
more and more
one.

It is that *pity*
that awareness of our oneness
that is at the heart
of the growing concern
for justice and peace.

Henry Vaughan
foresaw this
so very long ago
when he added
that he believed
that words like *alien* and *stranger*
would disappear.
He believed that those words
—indicating so often
a total lack of *pity*—
were notions
received from Cain
and his posterity
among us.
They feature
in the vocabulary of the killers and murderers
among us.
> We are many,
> though one,
> we are one
> though many!
> Doesn't that sound like the echo
> of the divine trinity:
> one
> though three,
> three
> though one?
Weren't we made
in their,
in that image?
Let us pray
that Jesus' compassion
may grow
in us.

38.

MULTIPLYING BY DIVIDING

John 6:1-15

He was standing in the valley
near the lake.
He saw them coming down
from the hills around,
thousands and thousands,
and he asked them:
how are we going to feed them?
He asked this to test them,
because he knew exactly
what he was going to do.
    Philip spoke about money
    they did not have,
    because nobody would be willing
    to give it to them.
    Andrew must have gone around
    to ask whether anybody
    had any food with him
    and they must have all answered:
    "no"
    with the exception of that small boy
    who said:

193

"yes,"
and who had shown him
five barley rolls
and two fishes,
all his mother had packed
for him
that morning.
Jesus took the bread,
Jesus took the fish,
he put them in their baskets
and said:
"hand it out!"
and they said:
"hand it out?"
and he said:
"hand it out!
Multiply it
by dividing it!"
They did
what he said
and they all got fed
and there were even twelve hampers full
left
after that.
Even for believing people
it is difficult to see
what happened that evening.
Did a new fish appear
every time they gave one out?
Did a new roll arise
every time they gave one away?
I don't say
that it was not that
what happened,
and yet I hope
that the miracle
was worked in a different way
that day.

There seems to be
another hint
about the miracle
that took place
that day!
> The hint is that boy
> who appears on the scene
> like an angel
> from heaven
> willing to share
> all he had got
> from his mother
> that morning.

When he heard
about the hunger,
when he heard
Jesus' demand for food,
his heart broke through
and instead of thinking
of himself
alone
he was willing
to share.
It is almost impossible
to imagine
that only that boy
had some food with him.
The others must have had
quite some rations with them
also.
But they were not willing
to share.
They kept their hands
on their pockets,
they kept their fish
under their shirt,
they had hidden their baskets
away.

And the miracle was
that at the moment
when Jesus started to multiply
the lunch-parcel
of that small boy
among them
by dividing it,
their hearts too broke through
just like the heart of that boy,
and they shared,
and there was plenty
left.
I hope it was
that type of miracle
that took place
because that is the type of miracle
we need
in our world
and in this country.
Let me explain to you
why.
Food is at the moment
multiplied
all over the world.
According to the reports
of the World Food Organization
the food-production
will increase
with 2.2 percent every year
up to the year
2000.
In global terms
there is no food problem.
Production is growing
faster
than the population growth
and yet each year
there are more malnourished people
than the year before,

because so many have *no access*
to that food.
They have no means to buy it.
At the moment there are
400 million to 600 million
malnourished people in the world.
Fifteen thousand people
are estimated to die each day
of starvation,
or of malnutrition-related causes.
    Yet,
        one third of all the cereals
        produced in the world,
        one third of all the grain,
        is used to feed the cattle
        for the meat
        of the rich.
There is more and more bread
in the basket
all the time.
The loaves are multiplying
at great speed
but there is no willingness
to divide,
there is no willingness
to break,
there is no willingness
to share,
there is no willingness
to have one's heart broken
like the heart of that small boy
did.
    A very well known man,
    Jim Wallis,
    who has been active
    for years
    in all kinds of movements
    for justice
    and peace,

for shelter
and food
for all,
recently wrote
that he felt
that what the world really needs
is *preaching*.
Preaching that would make
the gospel known
in our historical context
with a strong emphasis
on conversion.
He wrote:
"I am drawn these days
to preaching events
more than to conferences and workshops,
to revivals
more than to seminars,
to sermons
more than to lectures."
The bread is there,
the fish plentiful,
techniques improve,
expertise grows,
but the moral willingness to share,
the change of heart,
that must have struck
that crowd in front of Jesus
that day,
where is it among us
in our days?

39.

TO TAKE HIM AS OUR BREAD

John 6:24–35

They had come back.
Again they surrounded him,
with eager eyes
and ready stomachs.
He looked around and said:
I know why you come to me
again, not because of me
but because of the bread
I gave you:

>you want more bread,
>you want more fish,
>you want more food.

They watched him
with even more eager eyes
and the most hungry ones
must have already felt
the water
gush into their mouths.

>Once more he looked around
>and said:
>I am not going to give you
>that bread any more.

199

I am the bread of life,
take me as your bread.
They must have been unable
to understand
what he meant
and I wonder whether we really
do understand
after the two thousand years
that separate us
from those words.
  All the same
  the very language we use
  after those two thousand years
  might still have something
  from the bread
  he spoke about.
In English we sometimes
say
that something,
an attitude or a skill
is like *bread and butter*
to someone.
It means that she or he
is so accustomed to it
that it has become
a second or even a first nature
to her or to him.
  That is what
  he must have meant
  when he told them
  take *me*,
  take *me*,
  as your bread
  in life.
  Take *me*,
  take *me*,
  as the bread
  the Father is sending
  from heaven.

Take me
as the foundation
in your life.
Take me
as the principle
for your life
from day to day,
from hour to hour.
> If we take him
> in that way
> as our bread and butter in life
> we would choose always
> what is good for the world,
> what is good for humanity,
> what is good for all of us.

It would mean
that our work for peace
in the world and in our lives
would no longer be
a mere pious desire
or the subject for a clever workshop,
but a task that asks our effort.
> It would mean
> that the hunger in the world
> would no longer be
> an incident in the margin of our lives,
> or the topic of a naive social analysis
> but a challenge
> to provide the bread
> they were looking for
> —and so many are looking for—
> every day
> in the hands of all.

It would mean
that we would enter
the mercy and sadness
he had
because of our situation
in this world.

To enter into that mercy,
to enter into that sadness
would make us like him,
voices for the voiceless,
sufferers for peace,
organizers of justice,
chasers of evil,
healers of wounds.
Just imagine that we
who, without too much hesitation,
call ourselves
with his name
would be like that.
Making *him*
our bread
in life.

40.

OUR GOOD-BAD MIXTURE

John 6:41–51

Dear brothers and sisters
I am very glad to see you here again,
safe and sound,
but I am very sorry
that the main body of our community,
the students,
have been chased away.*
        There is a very old heresy
        called the manichean heresy.
        Maybe not very many of you
        ever heard that name,
        but that does not make you
        escape from its evil influence.
        It is a teaching
        according to which
        things, influences, and people
        in this world
        are *either* good *or* bad,
        either light *or* dark.
        It is a doctrine that divides society,
        that divides ourselves,

203

into those who are from God
and those who are from the devil.
Brothers and sisters,
let us be honest and frank
and let us ask ourselves
whether we have not been doing that
over this last week,
which has been for thousands and thousands
in this town
a horrifying one.
Is it not what we saw others do,
while they were plundering and condemning,
while they were judging and calling names.

You cannot do that
as a follower of Christ,
you cannot do that
if you are aware of the situation
in which we live.
Jesus' analysis of all creation
and of all society
is not
that some is good
and some is evil.
According to him
all is good,
all is fallen,
and all is in need of
redemption.
Don't you remember
how his disciples suggested to him
to eradicate ruthlessly
a village that had closed its gates
to him?
He told them:
you don't understand
my Spirit,
you don't understand
who I am.

Did you forget
how those same disciples suggested to him
to uproot all the evil
in the *shamba*† of this world
and how he looked at them
and said:
how would I be able to do that
without uprooting all the good
at the same time:
and they thought about themselves,
how they had been torn apart
if he would have uprooted the evil in them
and they did not have any further question
any more.
Do you remember
how he prayed to his father
while they nailed him on the cross:
please, Father, don't look at them,
they don't know what they are doing.
We are telling each other
gruesome stories
about the last days
and it is true
that gruesome things
did happen.
But was that gruesomeness
not set off
by good things also:
tact,
friendliness,
kindness,
care,
friendship,
and love?
Didn't I see with my own eyes
how a soldier
who had been bullying
hundreds of students

on their way out
suddenly put his gun down
to help a crippled student
who had fallen from his crutches
on the pavement
and who like
a beetle on its back
was unable to get up?

In 1945
a piece of brown packing paper was found
by an American soldier
near the dead body of a child
in Ravensbrueck,
a concentration camp
where 92,000 women and children died.
It read:

O Lord, remember not only the men and women
of good will,
but also those of ill will.
But do not only remember
the suffering they have inflicted on us,
remember the fruits we bought thanks to this suffering
our comradeship, our loyalty, our humility
the courage, the generosity
the greatness of heart which has grown out of all this.
And when they come to judgment
let all the fruits that we have borne
be their forgiveness.
Amen, amen, amen.

In the gospel of today
Jesus asks us
to let him be our bread,
to allow him to be
the substance of a new life,
every day.
We are here
to let him do that,
we are eating his bread,
we are eating him.

But we all know
that we fall so short,
so terribly short
of the life
he wants to live
in us.
His Spirit is not yet set free
in us,
we continue
complaining about him.
> That is how we are
> and aren't those others
> like us?
> That type of reflection
> must have been the reason
> that Paul wrote
> in the letter to the Ephesians
> today:
>> "Never have grudges against others,
>> or lose your temper,
>> or raise your voice to anybody,
>> or call each other names,
>> or allow any sort of spitefulness.
>> Be friends with one another,
>> and kind,
>> forgiving each other as readily
>> as God forgave you in Christ."
That does, however, not mean
that forgiveness
should be our only word
or our only attitude.
> It was not Christ's only word,
> nor his only attitude.
We should fight
with all the good in us
our evil.
We should fight
with all the good in our community
its evil.

We should try to establish justice
for all
against all the injustice
around us and in us
so that peace,
real peace
may prevail.

* This sermon was given a week after an attempted coup in Kenya. Part of the battle raged around Saint Paul's Chapel situated in the Main Campus next to the National Radio and Television Station which was occupied by rebels and reconquered by the army. Some of the students were said to have died in the crossfire. The day after the coup-attempt they were all sent home to report to their local chiefs. On the day of the coup-attempt there had been considerable looting in the town.

† *Shamba*: field, garden.

41.

HER ROLE
IN HUMAN HISTORY

Luke 1: 39–56

It is strange
that about thirty years ago
Pope Pius XII
decided to announce
solemnly
the assumption of Mary
into heaven.
> It was strange
> because for most Christians
> this assumption
> did not come as anything new.
> They had been believing this
> from the beginning,
> they had been celebrating that feast
> for centuries
> and centuries.
Experts have been asking themselves
why did Pope Pius XII
decide to do it?

There are many answers,
but one of the answers
has something to do
with what Pope Pius XII
had gone through himself
during his lifetime.
It was his way
of reacting to the horrible things
that had happened in his days.

> A first world war with 10 million dead,
> a revolution in Russia costing 40 million lives,
> a holocaust in which millions of Jews were murdered,
> a second world war with 50 million dead,
> those killed by two atomic bombs included.
> Those were only the dead.
> Whoever counted
> the millions and millions
> tortured and wounded,
> traumatized and handicapped
> for life?

All those facts
had been documented
in photographs and films,
in drawings and statistics,
human bodies
beaten,
starving,
dying,
dehumanized.

> And didn't we see here in this town
> recently
> the trucks that came to pick up
> the dead,
> one on top of another,
> on the way to the city mortuaries?

All people
who seemed to have lived and died
for nothing,
without reason,
without cause.

It is in that context
that Pope Pius XII
wanted to say something,
not only about the body
of
the mother of God,
but also about
all human bodies,
because what happened to her
will happen to all of us:
we will be taken up
with our bodies.
He must have hoped
that through this celebration
our respect
for the human body
and for the personal history
of each human person
would grow in us.
It is in that way
that he protested
against the maltreatment
of the bodies of others
by beating,
torture,
electric shocks,
or by using them
for self-satisfaction only.
It is in that way
that he wanted to teach us
how important
our own bodies
should be to ourselves.
There are too many of us
who treat our bodies
—to be taken up
in eternal glory—
badly.
Who poison the body
by too much drink;

who poison it
by too much tar and nicotine;
who overcharge it,
by too much work,
a too tight schedule
and an overfull diary.
>   There are too many of us
>   who are ashamed of our bodies
>   who do not seem to feel at home in the body,
>   who dislike or even hate it,
>   who consider it low and animal-like,
>   something to be hidden always.
Doctors and psychiatrists
nowadays even say
that these wrong attitudes to the body
might be the cause of sicknesses
like cancer.
>   Celebrating the feast of today
>   teaches us
>   that we will be taken up
>   *as we are*
>   with our bodily nature,
>   with our concrete personal history.
>   We will not be souls,
>   nor angels,
>   nor ghosts,
>   nor spirits.
>   We will be ourselves,
>   everything remains.
>   We cannot imagine it,
>   of course not,
>   but all our talk
>   about heaven,
>   about the soul in bliss,
>   about the glorified body,
>   about the glory of heaven,
>   about the assumption of the Blessed Virgin Mary
>   is nothing but saying:
>   this person
>   is *not* lost.

Mary was not lost,
   she did not disappear,
   she did not fall into nothingness,
   she who had carried God's one in her womb
   and after his death in her lap.
That is what she had understood
already
when she was singing her "magnificat"
in the gospel reading of today:
she would be praised forever,
she would be remembered forever,
she would live forever
because of the role
she played
in human history.
   So will we,
   so will the others
   forever
   and ever.

42.

HIS STORY ABOUT US

John 6: 60–69

All of us have had
difficult weeks
and the difficulties
seem not to be over as yet.
> We talk very much
> about what happened.
> We all have our story,
> we all have caught and explained
> those events
> in words.
> Everybody has her story,
> everybody has his story.
It is obvious
that those stories,
that those words
are important.
> As long as we are in panic
> we cannot say anything at all;
> as long as things are not yet settled
> we are looking for words,
> we don't know what to say.

An incident,
a car accident,
a sudden development,
a military coup,
something terrific,
something lovable,
are not understood by us,
are not part of us,
as long as we cannot tell
their story,
or sing
their song.
      We don't only tell stories
      about ourselves,
      about what happened to us.
      We also tell stories
      about others,
      about what happened to them,
      explaining them,
      how we see them
      from within our experience.
      How often have we said,
      hearing others tell
      their story about us:
      "Is that how you see it,
      is that how you see me?
      Amazing,
      I have never thought about it,
      about myself
      like that!"
That is what Jesus
had done to them.
He had told them
how he related to God
and how they should relate to God;
he had told them
how he felt about them,
and how they should feel about each other.

He had made it clear to them
what they could expect,
and how it all would end.
He had insisted
that they should change,
and take his life and person
so much as a model,
that he would be
—so to speak—
like bread to them.
        They had listened
        to his story
        all of them.
        Their reactions
        were very different.
        Some simply did not believe him,
        they walked away,
        saying:
        no thank you!
        or even worse:
        what nonsense!
Others did not only
not believe,
they said:
this has to stop,
he has to disappear!
They felt threatened,
they were rich or influential
and they planned
to betray and kill him.
        In the end
        he was almost alone;
        there were still the twelve
        and he asked them too:
        what about you?
        do you want to go away too?
        It was Peter who answered
        and said:

where shall we go,
we have heard your story about us,
and we believe,
you are the holy one,
the one from God.
Every Sunday,
every day of our life,
every hour
we are confronted
with his story
about our lives
in a world
where this story
is not accepted at all.
 Do we believe
 that one day
 we will forgive,
 as he told us
 we can do?
Do we believe
that one day
our bread will be broken
and shared,
as he told us
we shall do?
 Do we believe
 that one day
 God will be all
 in everyone,
 as he promised us
 in one of his tales?
Do we believe
in the coming
of the Kingdom
about which he told us
in story after story;
or are we inclined to say;
in fairy-tale after fairy-tale?

In the first reading of today
Joshua
gathered all of them together
at Shechem
and he asked them
whether they were going to remain faithful
to the Lord,
to the stories about their origin,
and about the meaning of their existence.
"If you don't,"
he said:
"Choose another story,
choose other words."
They looked at each other,
they looked at him,
and notwithstanding
all the difficulties
and hesitations
they retold their story
about their God,
and their liberation,
about the wonders,
and the way they had come
so far,
and they believed
once more.

43.

UNHEALTHY RITES

Mark 7: 1–8, 14–15, 21–23

It is already late in the evening;
suddenly the phone rings in the chaplaincy
and a very anxious voice at the other side
asks:
"Father,
is your Mass still free tomorrow?"
The answer is:
"No, I am sorry,
there is an intention already."
"But, father,"
the voice at the other side pleads,
"Can't you do something about it?
It is the anniversary
of the death
of my father
and we have been having a Mass
all the years after his death
on the day of his passing away.
It is just this time
that we forgot,
please, father.

It would be terrible
if there would be no Mass
this year,
terrible. . . .''
      You can hear the fear
      and even the terror
      in that voice at the other side.
      It is as if that deceased father
      was going to do something awful
      if that Mass
      were not said,
      as if he would come out of his tomb
      and spook around
      or cast a spell
      over the whole of the family.
You might laugh at this
and if you do,
it means
that such a thing would never happen to you;
but would you be able to admit
that similar fears
never overcome you?
Would you never, never be
in such a situation?
Are you trying to tell me
that you don't have rites and rituals,
gestures and words,
to try to control your life
and destiny?
      Do you never feel
      that you have to mumble a prayer,
                  touch an object,
                  swallow a bitter herb,
                  walk over a grave,
                  sprinkle some water,
                  spread some ashes,
                  grind some bone,
                  kill a chicken,

because otherwise. . . .
terrible things
will happen
to you?
All of us feel like that,
because all of us
would like to control and check
our neighbors,
nature,
and even God himself.
That is what those Pharisees too
tried to do.
By washing their hands,
by sprinkling their heads,
by dressing in a special way,
by wearing their hair in threshes,
by avoiding some,
by speaking to others,
by saying some prayers,
by laying on hands,
by sticking to hundreds and hundreds
of small little rules,
they tried to get a grip on themselves,
they tried to get a grip on their neighbors,
they tried to get a grip on their lives,
they tried to get a grip on nature,
they really tried to get a grip on God.
They thought they had caught him,
they thought that they knew what he would do,
they thought that they felt how he would react,
what he would reward,
what he would punish;
they had cut him to their own image,
they were sure that God was with them;
did they not fulfill all the conditions
they had set themselves?
Jesus disagreed,
but that is too mild a word;

Jesus threw out
totally
all their pretenses.
Jesus was not against law,
Jesus was not against rituals,
Jesus was not against rites,
Jesus was not against words,
and definitely not against the words of the Bible,
but he was against
any use of the law or the Bible,
he was against any rite or ritual,
that tried to control, to check, and to limit
God's love,
God's mercy,
God's grace
and consequently
human love,
human grace,
and human mercy.
That controlling,
that checking,
that limiting
is what we do
too often
by our rituals and rites!
God is with us
and not with the enemy:
and the weapons were blessed,
and the weapons are blessed
at the beginning of each crusade
to crush, to plunder, and to rape,
the infidels
in Syria and Israel,
in Iraq and Iran,
in South America and Europe,
in South East Asia and the States.
God is with us
and not with the others,

and the Bible was read and quoted
by Hitler and his company
in view of the
"Endloesung der Judenfrage"
and the Bible is read and quoted
to separate the whites from the blacks
and the coloreds from the rest.

God is with us
and not with sinners and devils
and witches are burned,
prostitutes despised,
dissidents tortured,
opponents put in prison.

God is with us
and the Bible is used
to formulate doctrines
that hinder our Christian intercommunion,
that oblige all priests to live like monks,
that absolutize impossible human marriage relations,
and that keep half of humankind
away from the altar.

In the gospel of today
Jesus turns himself
against all those laws and restrictions,
made by human beings,
that make us fearful
and afraid,
that restrict God's love
God's mercy, and God's grace,
and our love,
our mercy, and our grace
overlooking the real command,
he gave us all,
to love one another
unreservedly,
to share our bread
unrestrictedly.

So don't be afraid:

God's love and mercy and grace
is greater than any of our rites.
So don't use your rites,
your rituals,
your theology,
your use of the Bible,
your societal values,
to limit
God's love and mercy and grace
in you, yourself
either.
Amen.

44.

WHEN WORDS DON'T COME

Mark 7: 31–37

They brought him a deaf man
who had an impediment in his speech,
or in more usual terms
they brought him someone
who was deaf and dumb:
he could not hear,
he could not speak,
he was doubly handicapped.
>It was not so very long ago
>that Christians,
>followers of Jesus Christ,
>started
>—because of this story
>>of how Jesus touched
>>the ears of this man;
>>of how Jesus touched
>>the tongue of this man—
>institutes and homes
>to do something for those
>deaf and dumb.
>Those institutes were often called
>*institutes for the deaf and the dumb.*

225

About twenty years ago
we started to understand better and better
the relation
between most deafness
and most dumbness.
People could not speak
because they could not hear.
If you checked their organs of speech
they were all there, fully intact.
The deaf and the dumb were mostly
not doubly handicapped,
they could not hear,
they could not listen,
and not experiencing any sound
they could not make any sound either.
  After this discovery
  most of those institutes
  changed their name.
  They were no longer called
  institutes for the deaf and the dumb,
  but *institutes for the deaf*
  only.
If you cannot hear,
you cannot talk,
if you cannot listen,
you cannot speak.
  Jesus knew;
  he took that deaf and dumb man aside;
  first he touched his ears
  and then
  —was it still necessary?—
  his tongue.
  He heard and consequently,
  he spoke.
We can say this in general
but we can apply it also
to certain areas
in our lives.

Listen to the conversation
of the people around you;
listen to what they say
at the more critical situations
in life,
and you will notice
a great difference
between the older ones
and the younger ones.
The older ones,
the more traditional ones,
speak much more
about God and religion
than the younger ones.
Those modern ones
hardly speak in religious terms
at all.
They even seem to be embarrassed
if anyone in their company
does it.
They seem to be deaf
to that dimension
in human life.
How many in the world
in which we live are not deaf and dumb
when it comes
to God?

Didn't you feel often
hopeless and helpless
in a situation of great sorrow
or of great joy?
You felt you should say something
at this deathbed,
after that success,
during this sickness,
because of a healing,
and there you were,
with a mouth full of teeth,

with all your speech organs
intact,
looking for words,
that did not come,
searching for some light
that did not shine,
trying to make a sound
and you remained dumb.
It is as if religion
is on the way out.
It is as if religion
is forced into retreat
by modernity.
Would that mean
that we modern ones
lost the *aptitude*
to think, to speak,
and to talk
God-talk?
I wonder
whether our dumbness
is not due
to the fact
that we don't listen,
that we don't hear,
that we don't pray,
that we don't open our ears
to God
anymore.
We simply don't give ourselves
the time
for that.
We work and work,
and have no time
for any quiet.
Even Sunday,
in older times
a day to pray,

       to contemplate,
       to come to a rest,
       to re-evaluate,
       to re-assess,
       to listen and to hear,
       was changed into a day
       of being busy,
       of a trip,
       a consumer's day.
Something seems to be wrong
about the life-rhythm
we impose on ourselves.
We are interested in some selected activities
only:
       we have time to work,
       but no time to rest;
       we have time to amass,
       but no time to share;
       we have time to compete,
       but no time to unite;
       we have time to practice,
       but no time to celebrate;
       we have time to be busy,
       but no time to listen,
          no time to hear,
          no time for God,
          no time for our children,
          no time for our parents,
          no time for each other;
          no wonder
          that we are often
          dumb, and mute, and stupid.
Jesus met that man,
deaf and dumb,
in the bustle of the crowd,
with people all around him
busy with their affairs,
busy with their complaints,

busy with their work,
and he said
to that man
so deaf and therefore so dumb:
come with me for some quiet,
come with me for some peace
and it was then
when he was out of the crowd
in that quiet and peace
with Christ,
that the man
who had not been able to listen
and to hear
for all those years,
heard and listened
and, of course,
started to speak
very clearly.

>Let us allow ourselves
>to be taken out of the crowd
>by him
>to be able to listen
>and to speak.

45.

STRICKEN

Mark 8: 27–35

We are surrounded by people
who call themselves Christians.
Here in Nairobi
80 percent of the population is Christian,
50 percent are Protestants
30 percent are Catholics.
    None of them
    would have any difficulty
    with the question
    Jesus put to the disciples
    in the gospel of today:
    "Who do you say I am?"
    They all know the answer,
    they all know their catechism,
    they all know
    —more or less—
    the content of their creed.
    Without hesitation
    they would answer:
    you are the Christ,
    you are the Savior,

you are the Redeemer,
the light,
king of kings,
the prince of peace.
They are all orthodox
in the confession of their faith,
they are all faithful disciples
as far as doctrine
is concerned.
When it comes
to the second issue
in the gospel of today,
when it comes to the challenge
to follow him,
not only to be his student,
but his follower,
aren't we then
too often just like Peter,
who said: *no*
no, not that,
no, not your way,
no, not your lifestyle,
and couldn't Christ turn to all of us,
saying:
>   *satan*,
>   which means
>   adversary,
>   opponent,
>   saboteur,
>   contradictor,
>   dissident,
>   blocker of my work?
And he added
unconditionally:
if you want to be my follower
you have to go my way!
>   All this we heard,
>   all this we know,

all this we have heard but too often,
all this we know but too well,
what does it mean?
We have all kinds of traditional terms
to indicate
what it means,
we speak about him carrying
the sins of the world.
We speak about him
being the lamb of God.
We speak of him
dying for our sins.

    Let us try today
    to understand
    and to feel
    more profoundly
    what all this means.
To understand it better
and to feel it better,
we should be aware
of those among us
who at the moment
are carrying the sins of the world
because it is with them
that Jesus seems to identify himself.
We should try to find out
whether there are *now*
lambs of God
carrying our sins
among us.

    When you go in the evening
    to the General Post Office
    you might find there
    some girls.
    They are not always there,
    because very often they are chased away
    by the town-*askaris**
    with their dogs.

They are sometimes very young,
about 13 or 14 years old;
they wear
what they think to be
glamorous dresses,
though you can see
that nobody ever taught them
how to dress.
Their faces are made up
in an undecorous way,
the creams and the powders crackle
and fall off. . . .
They are despised by everybody,
though they are picked up now and then,
in the dark of the night.
They are not like that
because they like it.
They are like that
because they need money.
They would like to escape,
and when they are a bit older
they try to escape,
but they cannot,
some of them say
that they feel trapped
in a pit,
a very dark and deep pit,
that gets deeper and deeper
every day,
and the light at the top
is getting
dimmer and dimmer.
All of us
would call them sinners,
and they are
in the sense
that they are carrying
the whole load of the sin

        of the society
        in which they live.
Do you see that?
Can you see that?
Are you willing to see that?
        You might say
        that all the sin
        in this society
        is carried and absorbed
        by them.
They are what they are
because of the greed,
because of the heartlessness,
because of the hard-heartedness,
because of the injustices,
because of the inequalities,
because of the evil behavior
of our society.
        It would definitely be an exaggeration
        to say
        that they are innocent lambs,
        but they do carry the sins of this world,
        they do carry the sins of our world,
        they do carry your sins and mine!
And, of course,
they are lambs of God.
        Did you ever realize
        that so much the prophet Isaiah
        said of his oppressed people
        could be said of them:
        "Surely they have borne our griefs
        and carried our sorrows
        yet we esteemed them as stricken,
        smitten by God and afflicted.
        They were oppressed and afflicted,
        yet they opened not their mouths,
        like lambs they are led to the slaughter,
        like sheep that before their shearers are dumb,

so they opened not their mouths.
By oppression and judgment
they were taken away
and as for their generation
who cared a hoot that they were cut off out of the land
of the living,
stricken for the transgressions
of their people?'' (Isaiah 53)
Brothers and sisters,
Jesus Christ identified himself
with them.
He became like them,
he sat down with them,
he ate with them,
he had pity on them,
and it was in that way,
through his respect for them,
that he judged and condemned
the evil of the world
in which they lived.

    The elders
    understood
    and they fumed;
    the priests
    understood
    and they cursed,
    the scribes
    understood
    and shouted: blasphemy.
    They all understood,
    they grasped his logic,
    they felt his attitude
    and they decided
    to kill.
That is what they did,
they murdered him
in a very appropriate way,
in the company
of two criminals.

That is what they did not do,
because he rose
from the death
they inflicted on him.
        He came back,
        proving that evil
        was overcome,
        proving that evil
        can be overcome,
        that another life
        is possible.
        He carried all sins
        out of this world
        and returned
        to start a new life.
        We are asked
        not only to *know*,
        but to *follow*,
        not only to be a disciple
        but a follower!
        Struggling with him
        in ourselves *now*
        and in this world *here*
        against the greed,
        the heartlessness,
        the hard-heartedness,
        the injustices,
        the evil behavior,
        that threaten all of us.
"If anyone wants to be a follower of mine,
let him renounce himself
and take up his cross
and follow me!"

* *Askaris*: municipal vigilants.

46.

HE TOOK A CHILD

Mark 9:30–37

They could not have been walking
with him.
They must have been walking
behind him
or maybe in front of him.
    They were discussing
    their relations with him.
    They were discussing
    their importance
    according to him.
We don't know
what they said,
but we can guess
what they said.
    Peter said:
    of course,
    without any doubt:
    I am the most important,
    didn't he call me
    rock
    on which he is going to build
    that community of his?

John said:
I am sorry for you;
what you say might be true
but that is only a question
of administrative bureaucracy;
the fact that you might be a better administrator
does not make you
the most important one.
You should look
for something else,
you should look
for something more important,
you should look
for his *love*
and then . . .
he loves me most.

      Then Judas spoke;
      he said:
      the most important fellow
      is the one with the money,
      you don't need to be a Marxist,
      nor a capitalist
      to know that;
      the world is ruled by money
      and to whom did he entrust
      his money,
      to me
      and that is why . . . !
Philip spoke;
he said:
all that is very nice,
but you remember
when he had that catering-problem
in the desert
with all those thousands
when nobody knew what to do,
he himself included,
he turned to me
to ask for *advice*;

I am sorry for you,
it was me.
>He must have walked
>ahead of them
>or behind them
>during that conversation,
>having his thoughts,
>having his sentiments
>while they had theirs.
He spoke about
being delivered
into the hands of men;
>they spoke
>about how others
>would be delivered
>to them;
he spoke about saving others;
carrying their plight;
they spoke about themselves
in the small circles
of their personal lives;
>he spoke about
>being a servant,
>they spoke about
>being a master.
At first sight
of course
their discussion
was very pious.
They spoke about their relation
to him;
they spoke about their relation
to God.
>Peter spoke about
>Jesus' trust in him
>while beating his
>enormous chest.
John spoke about
Jesus' love,

and he pointed
at his heart.
    Jude shook
    Jesus'purse
    and said:
    this is the thing
    that counts.
Philip spoke
about Jesus' appreciation
for his judgment and flair.
    They were in fact
    all speaking
    about themselves.
    They were not only speaking,
    they were fighting,
    there was tension,
    there was war.
    I don't even know
    whether their hands
    did not feel for their knives
    and their swords
    under their dress.
He must have walked
ahead of them
or behind them
during that conversation;
he could not have walked with
them
that time.
    When I came to the United States
    some days ago*
    I could not sleep very well
    because of jet-lag.
    I woke up at odd hours
    and during those odd hours
    I switched on the TV
    in the room
    of the Wooster Inn
    where I stayed.

I was amazed to find people
preaching in the middle of the night
about Jesus,
and I was even more amazed
about the message,
because that message
seemed to me to be
a mere continuation
of the type of competitive fight
those disciples had
so very long
ago.
It was all about "I":
I standing in front of my savior,
I being anointed,
I being in a holy place,
I with my loins girded,
I with my breastplate of faith,
I with my sword of truth,
I feeling so fine;
    very pious,
    very scriptural,
    and in the end
    even Judas' purse
    and the money
    are not forgotten!
They arrived at Capernaum,
they arrived at his house,
they went inside,
they washed their feet,
they sat down.
He asked them:
what were you speaking about,
what were you shouting about,
what was all the noise about
when I walked behind you,
when you walked in front of me?
    There was no answer,
    they looked at each other,

they felt ashamed,
they felt stupid,
they realized he knew.
When there had been a silence
for quite some minutes,
he stood up,
he went to the door,
he disappeared,
leaving them, speechless, behind.
They did not even dare
to look at each other.
He came back,
he had a child by the hand,
one he had found in the street.
A small girl,
with a running nose
and pitchblack eyes.
He put the girl
in the middle of their circle
and he said:
"Do you see her?"
Of course they did.
He put his hands on her,
he greeted her,
he kissed her
and said:
"Whoever receives a child
like this one,
breaking open
the circle in which
she or he lived
is receiving
ME
and not only me
but the one who sent me
also."
He looked at them
and he sent the girl
around in their circle.

I don't know what they did:
>Peter gave her a pat
>on her shoulders,
>John kissed her
>on both her cheeks;
>Judas gave her a coin,
>and Philip put her
>on his knee.

If they received,
that evening,
that small girl
in all sincerity
they must have been filled
—according to his word—
with God's self
and a question like
"Who is the most important?"
did not make any sense any more.

* This reflection was given in the McGaw Chapel of Wooster College, Ohio, October 10, 1982.

47.

BELONGING TO HIM

Mark 9:38–43, 47–48

I was at the General Post Office
here in town.
I had bought some stamps.
I had to put them on my letters.
I walked to the other side of the hall
where a kind of very high table
is placed
so that you can put stamps
and do things like that
without sitting down,
keeping you on the move.
      Next to me two ladies
      were talking to each other.
      I did not want to listen in,
      but I could not help it;
      they spoke rather loudly.
      I don't know their complete conversation;
      I only heard one say:
      "You know,
      they are Catholics of course,
      they think that they have the truth,

the way,
and the life,
they have no time for us.''
''Yes,''
I heard the other answer.
''Silly, isn't it?''
and after that I heard nothing
anymore,
they walked out into the street
and I posted my letters.
It is already long ago,
most probably more than two years,
and yet
those two voices
still ring in my ears
as if I am just coming
from the post office.
When I prepared
this reflection
and was looking for a relevant beginning
to the readings of today,
suddenly that incident
came into my mind.
Why,
I don't know,
how,
I don't know
either,
but it did.
John belongs obviously to Jesus
in the gospel of today,
he belongs to his circle,
to his intimates.
One tells of John,
in fact it is John himself
who tells it,
that he would always
sit next to Jesus
as close as possible,

like a child
next to his father,
like a schoolgirl
next to her beloved teacher.
John was happy
with his position,
he was proud of it,
and he was jealous.
He would not like
anyone
to take his place.
It is in the gospel of today
that this same John
who had noticed
that others unknown to him,
unknown to Jesus,
as far as John knew,
used the name of Jesus
to work miracles
and to cast out devils.
John was horrified
and he went to Jesus
to tell him so.
He said:
I saw a man
who is not one of us,
who does not belong to our circle,
who does not belong to your intimates
or friends,
cast out devils
using your name.
John was very upset,
all exclusiveness
seemed to be gone.
If a thing like this
were permitted,
what was the use
of belonging
to Jesus' group?

John wanted to restrict
Jesus' influence
to their one group,
to their one party,
to their one option,
to their one company.
And the others?
Woe to them!
Then Jesus speaks,
and he made his point
very clear:
"Don't stop those others,
they are working miracles;
if they are doing good,
they must be all right."
It was in that way
that he opened John's perspective;
it was in that way
that he broke through the exclusiveness
of all those small groups of believers
who think that they have exclusive rights,
special access to the full truth,
special relation to divine power
and so on.
To make it even clearer,
Jesus makes his second remark
about that simplest of things
a cup of water,
saying
anyone who would give you
a cup of water
whether he belongs to us or not
will certainly
not lose his reward.
John wanted to close off,
John wanted to insulate,
John wanted to close the circle,
John had no respect for others
who according to him
had little or no faith.

Jesus continued
adding:
"If you would be an obstacle
to the faith and insight
of those others,
you better be thrown
into the sea
with a millstone
around your neck."
  Brothers and sisters,
  do you hear
  what Jesus said,
  do you see how he might be talking to us,
  do you hear how he might be talking to you?
To us,
who so often look down
on others
because they don't believe in Jesus,
because they don't believe in Jesus in our way;
to all those Catholics
or Protestants
who claim:
we are the chosen ones,
we are the elected ones,
we are the intimates,
we are the saved ones,
we are the knowers,
the exclusive possessors
of the path and the life and the truth?
  Even the second reading of today
  says something
  about that strange exclusive attitude
  of ours.
You heard the second reading.
It is about the rich,
it is about us.
James does not blame the rich
for being rich.
He blames them
not for that,

he blames them
for something else;
he blames them
for isolating themselves;
he blames them
for the false security they live in;
he blames them
for the small exclusive world
in which they live,
not open to others,
not thinking of others,
being on their own,
being a divisive element
in the world
in which they live.
He wrote:

> Start crying,
> start weeping,
> open your heart,
> be with the others,
> do not condemn them,
> do not kill them,
> share!

The sharing meant here
is not only giving;
giving is easy,
it is also receiving;
it is not only speaking;
speaking leaves you master,
it is also listening.

> If only the whole people of the Lord
> would be prophets,
> *that is the giving*;
> and the Lord gave his Spirit
> to them all,
> *that is the receiving.*
> Amen.

48.

ONE BODY

Mark 10:2–12

Today is the day
that many preachers feel
that the truth should be said
about our human relationships,
especially in married life.
It should.
>   It often means
>   that all divorce
>   will be condemned
>   by those who know least
>   about the causes
>   of the break
>   in this type
>   of human relationships.
Celibate priests,
unmarried as they are,
can talk with ease
about what strikes others
when they dare to risk
a relation and intimacy
that those priests themselves
are not allowed to try.

251

Isn't it always a temptation
to gloat
when others fail
while trying to do something
you yourself are not allowed to try,
or do not dare to do?
The listeners
in the churches of those priests
might get very hurt
when they hear
how they themselves
and others they know
are condemned
for difficulties
that often
are not of their making.
On one hand those priests
seem to extend
what Jesus said
to cases
he does not speak about
at all.
On the other hand
those priests
seem to restrict
what Jesus said
to relations
in marriage alone.
They extend it.
Of course, Jesus is
against any break in love,
in the case of two
who married each other.
That is why he says:
"A man is not allowed
to chase his wife away
through a small handwritten note
reading:

get out,
you are free to do
what you want,
because I do not want
you
anymore!''
He is against
that procedure,
once allowed,
because of their hardness of heart
and their unteachability,
as it reduces
the woman
to the rank of the disposables
you can get rid of
at your convenience.
    He is against it,
    because according to him
    our human relations
    should be loving and respectful.
Brother or sister,
if that love
and respect
are the norm,
would it then not be possible
that in view of that love
and respect,
certain marriages,
that were a mistake,
certain marriages
that turned sour,
because of an ever-growing incompatibility
of the two in question,
are declared
null and void?
    Those priests restrict
    what Jesus said,
    maybe,

too much
to marriage relations
only.
Jesus seems to speak
in a larger context
when he says:
"God made them male and female,
the two are one!"
      Jesus seems to speak
      about all those situations
      where men have chased
      women.
Jesus seems to condemn
all the onesidedness
when only one approach,
the male one,
is pushed
to the extent
that the other approach,
the female one,
is oppressed.
      Jesus seems to condemn
      the male-oriented,
      the male-dominated world
      (and church),
      in which we try
      to live.
"They should be
no longer two,
they should be one,
as God created them,
male and female,
in the image
of God."
      The rich relationships
      between man and woman,
      as exemplified
      in a good and harmonious marriage,

and its fertility,
are the model
for the world
to come
according to him.
Amen.

49.

NOT ONLY AT HOME

Mark 10: 17–30

A man runs up to Jesus.
He was young;
older men do not run,
they might jog,
but that is not the same
as running.
> He knelt down in front of Jesus
> in a cloud of dust,
> and he asked Jesus,
> who must have been very surprised
> by his eagerness
> and enthusiasm:
> "What should I do
> to live eternally?"
Jesus looked at him,
he looked once more,
and then he recommended
to him
all the normal household virtues:
> do not murder,
> do not commit adultery,
> do not steal,

do not accuse falsely,
do not deceive,
and honor your father and your mother.
The youngster looked at him
and said:
"But that is what I have been doing
up to now!"
Jesus looked at him again,
and now he looked with more understanding
about what went on
in the heart and the mind of that young man,
and looking at him
with love,
remembering how he himself
had lived that virtuous homely life
with Joseph and Mary,
with breakfast and lunch,
with his family and his friends,
with the folks at home
for thirty solid years
in Nazareth;
he remembered too
how he had exchanged
that homely life
for something else.
He remembered the day
that he too had thought
—just like the young man,
who was now kneeling in front of him—
that there was more to life,
that there was another obedience,
another commitment
asked of him,
and he said:
"There is one more thing
you should do.
Go and sell all you have,
give it away to the poor
just as I did,

and come and follow
me!''
    The young man's face
    started to fall
    He thought,
        not so much of his money
        his chariot,
        and the amount of his savings
        in the bank,
    he thought of that too,
    I suppose,
    but he thought also
    of his father and his mother,
    of his friends at home,
    of the open fire
    and the food and the drinks,
    about their small intimate circle
    with doors and windows
    securely closed.
    He sighed,
    he sighed very deeply,
    and he went,
    without a greeting,
    not even looking up
    anymore.
    Jesus must have understood.
    Hadn't he experienced
    that same difficulty
    when he left
    his father and mother,
    his family and friends,
    his house and his village
    for the kingdom of God?
And he said,
thinking of himself,
"How difficult it is,
for the rich
to choose
for the kingdom of God!''

A difficulty
all of us meet in life,
because all of us,
you and me,
are so tightly knit up
with our worries and joys at home,
that we often aren't prepared at all
to open up
to those issues that concern
the kingdom of God
in this world:

> the issues of justice and peace,
> of love for all,
> your enemies included
> the issues of weapons and threats
> and a brotherhood
> for all people.

We should live
all the virtues
Jesus practiced at home.
That is what he asked
that young man to do,
but we should not forget
that he asked him too
to look further
than that.

50.

HIS TYPE OF LEADERSHIP

Mark 10: 33–45

That morning
James and John
went to him.
> They went
> when they thought they would be alone.
> They went,
> while the others did not see them,
> while the others did not hear them.

They asked him
a very simple question.
They asked him
whether they would be allowed
to rule with him;
they asked him
to be allowed
to sit at his right
and at his left
side.
> When the others heard
> what had happened,
> they were very upset
> and very angry.

They were indignant,
the reason being, of course,
that they all would have liked
to ask him
that very same question,
but they had not dared.
When we hear this story
we might be surprised
and indignant too.
How could people
who were so close to him
ask a question like that?
How could they be
so egoistic,
so full of self,
so out for power and glory,
so pushy in his company?
We forget,
very comfortably
that all our lives long
we have been doing the same thing
in the company of human beings
and in the company of God.
As a child we asked
and maybe even prayed:
I want an ice-cream,
I want a bicycle,
I want this,
I want that,
overlooking totally
our brothers and sisters
not to speak about
all the other children.
As a grown-up we asked
and definitely prayed
for promotion:
"Dear Sir,
considering my capacities
and my recent successful activities,

I am of the opinion
that you should agree with me
that I am an excellent appointee
for your vacant directorship . . . !''
Nevertheless
hearing about James
and John
we might be so surprised,
and so indignant,
that we project
without any further ado
our indignation
into the mind of Jesus.
That is not correct,
it is wrong,
because Jesus
does not seem to be
surprised
at all,
and he is definitely
not indignant.
He does *not* blame them
for asking their question.
Of course there should be leaders,
of course there should be guides,
of course there should be persons
willing to lead:
how would we be able
to survive
without them?
Isn't one of the difficulties
these days
that there is a lack
of good leadership?
Jesus does not blame them
for their request,
but he blames them
for their reason
for asking for an important function.

They wanted to be
in that high position
in order to rule;
they wanted to be
the boss
so that the others would serve them,
and Jesus said:
that is wrong.
Jesus said:
    "Whoever wants to rank first among you,
      must serve the needs of all."
And he asked them:
    "Are you willing to do that,
      are you willing to go through that pain,
      to go through that bath of pain?"
What are we looking for,
what are you looking for
when we,
when you and I,
look for promotion,
look for honor,
look for fame?
    Is it to be the boss,
    or is it to be the servant;
    is it to be the master,
    or is it to be the slave?
Jesus became our master
because he served us all.
    And even nowadays
    there are so many examples
    of that type of serving leadership
    amongst us.
Think of Maximilian Kolbe,
canonized last week,
who gave his life
to save the life
of a family-man.
    Think of Martin Luther King
    shot in the service of many.

Think of Archbishop Oscar Romero,
killed because he defended the poor.
    They went to the extreme,
    they were called to go to that extreme,
    how far do you go,
    how far do we go,
    in our service
    of the others?

51.

BARTIMEUS WAS DIFFERENT

Mark 10: 46–52

Jesus is on his way
to Jerusalem.
He is passing the town
of Jericho.
As usual a crowd is
surrounding him.
    He had told that crowd
    several times
    that he was going to be arrested,
    detained, and murdered
    in Jerusalem.
    They were not even interested
    in what he said.
    They were interested only
    in themselves.
    They surrounded him only
    to profit from him
    personally:
    the poor wanted his money;
    the deaf and the dumb
    wanted to be healed;

265

the ones with toothaches and headaches
wanted to be liberated
from their pain.
That was all.
They appreciated him
as a miracle worker.
They were not interested
in his intentions
to change the world,
to make it a better
and a more just place.
That is why
they all left him
at the moment that the money
was given,
or the miracle
had taken place.
As soon as the toothache
was over,
they rushed home
to continue
their normal lives;
as soon as they were not paralyzed
anymore
they walked away from him;
as soon as they could speak,
they ran to their friends and families
to tell all the stories
they had never been able
to tell before.

     While the crowd pushed
     against him,
     there was that blind beggar
     in the gutter of the street;
     he could not join the crowd,
     being blind.
     The only thing *he* could do
     was to shout,
     and that is what he did;

he shouted:
Jesus, Son of David, help me!
But the ones in the crowd
told him to shut up.
They did not want to open their circle
though Jesus spoke to them
about a general brotherhood of men,
about a general sisterhood,
about *undugu*,*
about *udada*,†
about loving each other,
as much as you love yourself.
They did not want to open their circle,
afraid that they might miss their chance
to be touched by Jesus.
But Jesus said:
did I hear anybody call me?
They said:
no,
nobody,
and again they pushed
to get nearer
to him.
The man,
Bartimeus by name,
shouted a second time:
Jesus, Son of David, help me!
Jesus said:
I heard him again,
open up your circle,
bring him here.
And though unwillingly
they opened their circle
and told the blind man:
he is asking for you.
Bartimeus jumped up,
losing his cloak and his stick,
and they guided him to Jesus
who asked:

what do you want from me?
Bartimeus said:
Please, let me see again!

Jesus said:
all right,
see again,
your faith has saved you!
Bartimeus saw,
and when Jesus saw
that Bartimeus
could see again,
he said:
go, you are healed,
expecting that Bartimeus
would do
what all the others had done
as soon as they were healed:
go and start their old life
again.
Bartimeus looked for his cloak
and his stick,
a stick he really did not need
anymore;
but Bartimeus did not go.
Bartimeus stayed
and followed him.
Bartimeus remained
with Jesus.

This miracle
of the blind man Bartimeus
is the last miracle told of Jesus
before his death on the cross.
It is the last one
in the gospels of Mark, Matthew, and Luke,
and it is the first one
in which a man healed
decides
to remain with Jesus,

to work with him
at a better,
at a more just world.
Bartimeus should be
our example.
People so often complain
about Christians,
about those touched by Jesus Christ.
They will say of Kenya:
70 percent baptized,
why is it
that people do not love each other
more,
why is it
that so much goes wrong
all the time?

> Is it not because too many of us,
> after having been touched by Jesus,
> go home again
> as if nothing had happened?
> That is what they all did
> in those crowds around Jesus,
> even asking for his death
> afterwards,
> when they thought him
> to be a loser
> and helpless.

Let us not be like that,
let us be like Bartimeus
who stayed with him
in his struggle
for justice
and love
and peace.
Amen.

* *Undugu*: brotherhood.
† *Udada*: sisterhood.

52.

ABOUT THE GOOD LIFE

Mark 12: 28-34

That man asked the deepest possible
question,
the final one,
the determining one,
the one all of us
have been asking
one time or another:
> which is the first of the commandments?
> what is the most important thing in life?
> what should we do to live well?
> what is the good life?

You know
how the answer to that question
seems to be *legio*,
a thousand,
a thousand different ones.
> You might even meet
> those different answers
> in your own family:
> you are a Catholic,
> your father is a Muslim,

your mother Church of Kenya,
your sister a Seventh-Day Adventist,
your son a Quaker,
and your daughter,
who knows what your daughter is?
The question was asked
by one of the scribes,
one of the learned ones of his time,
and if he was sincere in saying
that he did not know it
anymore,
he must have been
confused,
like so many of us
are confused.
        He asked Jesus
        and Jesus answered
        by saying
        one word
        only!
Jesus said:
"Listen!"
Jesus said:
"Hear!"
Jesus said:
"Open your ears!"
Jesus said:
"Listen!"
        And in that one word
        he had said it all.
That one word indicated
all the rest that followed.
That one word summed up
the love for God
and
the love for the other
and
the love for self.

You don't believe me?
Just think
of your everyday experience.
Is the one who loves you
not the one
who listens to you?
You have a difficulty,
you go to a doctor,
you go to a priest,
you go to a lawyer,
you go to a psychiatrist,
you go to your father,
you go to your mother,
you go to someone you thought to be
your friend;
    your problem is serious,
    your anxiety great,
    but they,
    they say
    that they have no time,
    that they are too busy,
    that you don't have the money,
    and even when they listen
    you see their eyes turn away
    from you
    in other directions,
    you feel their minds
    turn away,
    they do not love.
Think of yourself
when someone
you don't like
comes to you
not only to tell a story
but to make you
a participant
in her worries,
his anguish,
her sickness.

Do you ever listen,
really listen
when you don't love her,
when you don't like him?
Think of the moments
you found one
who listened,
really listened
endlessly to you:
is it not true
that all of us complain
that nobody seems to listen
to us?
That learned man,
that professor or so,
went to Jesus
and he asked
what is the most important thing in life?
And Jesus said:
Listen
to God;
listen
to your neighbor;
listen
to the source of life;
listen
to human life;
there is no commandment
greater than this,
because if you listen
life will be loved
and the consequences drawn.
You don't need much imagination,
you don't need much insight
to know and feel
that this is true.
If we listen to God
we will not fight together
in God's name.

If we listen to God
things will be shared.
If we listen to God
others will be heard too.
If we listen to God
the others will
hear us
also.

    If we listen to God
    God will be loved
    with all our heart,
    with all our soul,
    with all our mind,
    and with all our strength,
    and we will love our neighbor
    as ourselves.

Translate the word *love*
by *listen*
and you know what *love*
is about
and the "good" life
too.

53.

THE REAL THING

Mark 12: 38–44

He was sitting in the temple,
the place he called
the house of my Father.
He had spoken
about its discontinuation
on several occasions.
He had spoken
about its closure.
He had even spoken
about its destruction,
    but it still was
    the house,
    the old house
    of his Father.
He sat down somewhere
on the foot of the column
to take in more easily
the things that were happening
around him.
    The scene he saw
    was fantastic,

in as far as we can judge
from the reconstructions
made.
Very important people would suddenly appear
on the scene,
enormously rich merchants
who made their pilgrimage
to Jerusalem
from very far off countries
where they had become very rich.
They were lavishly dressed,
full of money,
who,
in view of their business interests
in Jerusalem,
were very willing
to deposit large sums of money,
in clanking silver and gold
in the offering boxes
before starting
their deals.

> Jesus looked at them,
> he listened to the noise
> of their money,
> from the foot of the pillar
> on which he sat,
> *and he was not impressed.*

Priests would appear
in a dress
that singled them out
from the common people
as much as possible.
When they appeared
the Jewish *wananchi**
gave way immediately.
The best places were evacuated,
pillows and cushions
were brought in,

to allow them to pray
after their seats
had been dusted and cleaned
by the servants
they brought with them,
to avoid
any kind of impurity.
      Jesus looked at them,
      he listened to the noise
      of their prayers,
      from the foot of the pillar
      on which he sat,
      and he was not impressed.
Scribes came in,
people who knew the law.
They knew it so well
because they had made it up
themselves
for the greatest part.
They would sit down
to listen to the legal difficulties
of those who were willing to pay
and who at the same time
were defenseless against the hypocritical
defenders and protectors of their rights.
They would listen
up to the moment that
the last penny of their victims,
often poor widows and disinherited orphans,
had been paid to them,
after they had sold
the last thing they had
in this world.
      Jesus looked at them,
      he listened to the noise
      of their voices and the scratching
      of their pens,
      and he was not impressed.

Others were very impressed.
They had come from all over the world,
to that temple.
It was there
that you could see life,
the real thing,
they said.
It was there
that human destiny
was decided,
they thought.
It was there
that the future was made.
> Up-country people,
> a little bit shy
> because they felt
> badly dressed
> and not at ease at all,
> gaped at those merchants,
> > those priests and
> > those scribes.
> Jesus looked at it all
> from the foot of the pillar
> on which he sat
> *and he was not impressed*
> *at all.*
Then she came in,
old and dried up,
wrinkled and sickly.
In her hands she carried
a handkerchief,
in that handkerchief
she was hiding something;
she went to the offering block.
> Jesus looked at her,
> but he did not say
> a word.
At the offering block
she opened her handkerchief,

and now one could see
what she had been hiding
up to then:
two copper coins,
all the money she had.
    She could have divided
    those two coins
    between her and the temple,
    one coin for each.
    She did not do that.
    She took both her coins
    and dropped them
    in the opening
    of the offering block,
    already pushed away
    by those others with
    their bags of gold and silver.
Jesus stood up,
he called his disciples together
and in between
all the silk and the gold,
the cassocks and copes,
mitres and crosiers,
the books and dusty papers,
he pointed her
out to them
and he said:
    she gave
    all she had.
    She was pure
    in her intentions.
    Look
    at what she did
    and forget about
    all the rest.
Very many of us
are very often
wondering about the things
we do in life.

"Was I really born,"
a housewife might sigh,
"to change the diapers of
my children?
Should not I do something
more important?"
            "Was I really born,"
            a never-promoted clerk might say,
            "to push papers
            all my life?
            Is that all there is
            to my existence?"
When we worry
like that,
and who doesn't,
we should remember
that scene in the temple,
where that simple act of love
was considered to be greater
than anything else
in this world:
the real and
decisive thing.
Amen.

* *Wananchi*: common people.

54.

THE END OF THIS WORLD

Mark 13: 24–32

The sun will be darkened,
the moon will fade,
time of distress.
> The gospel of today
> sounds at first hearing
> very threatening.
> There will be wars,
> there will be famines,
> there will be earthquakes,
> families will be ripped apart,
> there will be conflicts,
> there will be persecutions,
> there will be horrible things
> and those thirsting for justice
> will stand before judges.
Many people in our world
are full of that kind of
doom-thinking.
Very many people in this country
have been asking me:
don't you think
that the end is very near;

don't you think
that Jesus will return
very soon?
> Sometimes this leads
> to situations
> where some lose all courage.
> They are not open to any future
> anymore.
> They are not willing
> to continue life
> in view
> of that imminent end.

In certain countries in the North,
where the fog is always thicker
than here in the South,
where the darkness
lasts for weeks,
young people
even decided
not to have any children
any more.
> Having children
> in view of what,
> they say,
> to be roasted alive
> in an atomic explosion?

Yet,
brothers and sisters,
when you read the gospel,
even the short excerpt of today,
more carefully,
you will notice
that a gospel like the one today
is NOT
a gospel of doom
at all.
> Of course,
> it is a gospel
> about distress;

it is a gospel
about pain;
it is a gospel
about dying.
That distress, however,
is not the important thing,
that pain is not the end,
that dying is not the real sign.
Jesus makes that very clear
by the parable he adds.
In that parable
he brings us in front
of a tree
that lost all its leaves
during a drought
or during wintertime.
He invites us:
look well,
and you look
and you see
all over the tree
small brown buds
and you look at Jesus
and you say:
so what,
and Jesus says:
remain looking,
and then you see
movement,
change,
life,
the small buds open,
the brown surrounding leaves
give way,
they crack,
they bend,
they break
—to them disaster,
distress, the end—

and new life
is born,
a pale green shoot,
while the old protecting leaves
fall on the earth
to dry up
in a sun that is
darkening to them,
in a moon
that fades
for them.
          You might even use
          that more salient image
          of John,
          not bound to seasons
          like the parable
          today.
It is the image
in which Jesus compares
the whole of creation
to a woman giving birth.
          She is in pain,
          in terrible pain,
          but it would be nonsense
          to look only at her pain,
          saying:
          how horrible,
          what a distress,
          what a drama;
          because that pain
          is not the important thing,
          that distress
          is not the end.
          That pain is a sign
          of the new life
          to be born,
          and once born
          it will be forgotten
          very soon
          because of that new life.

Jesus
indicates to us
the way
in which we should look
at the crumbling of the old world
around us,
at the falling away
of so many things
we are accustomed to.
Jesus tells us
how to look at the conflicts,
the wars and starvation
and he says:
>   be careful,
>   don't get confused,
>   don't let them frighten you,
>   don't worry,
>   keep going
>   in the end
>   all will be fine.
He even added
that because of us
and our work
God will take care,
that the transitional time,
that the misery and distress
will be shortened.
>   Robert Muller
>   is an undersecretary
>   of the United Nations,
>   and he wrote
>   using practically the same kind of image:
>   "We are witnessing
>   a unique moment of evolution,
>   the birth of collective organs
>   in the human species.
>   For the first time
>   humankind is emerging
>   as a global organism
>   with a common bloodstream,

a central nervous system,
a shared heart,
a corporate brain,
and a common destiny.''
He said it
in a secular way.
The gospel uses
religious terms:
"And then they will see
the Son of man,
coming in the clouds
with great power and glory,
then too he will send angels
to gather together his chosen
from the four winds,
from the ends of the world
to the ends of heaven.''
Let us live
with his vision:
humanity in labor
to give birth,
in distress and pain,
to that human and divine
organism
of whom He
is the head.
Amen.

55.

A LINE OF KINGS

John 18: 33-37

Today,
the last Sunday of the year,
is the feast of Jesus Christ
King.
>It is a feast
>that can easily be misunderstood.
>It is a feast
>that is very often
>misunderstood.
>It is a feast
>that can cause difficulties.
>It is a feast
>that once was celebrated
>with gunshots in the morning,
>a military/ecclesiastical parade
>in the afternoon,
>with flags, trumpets, drums,
>the presentation of arms,
>and schoolchildren,
>singing and marching
>in their thousands.

287

In some countries
this feast of Christ King
is still celebrated
like that,
especially in those Catholic countries
that are ruled by soldiers
and dictators,
because those soldiers and dictators
need someone like that,
even if there is no king.
    Normally
    the presence of a king,
    a real old-fashioned king,
    means
    that others are not kings
    at all.
    In any country
    where a king rules
    no one else is allowed
    to use the title king,
    and even names like royal
    are sometimes completely exclusive.
    There can be only one king.
    Just as in other countries
    there can be only one president
    and no one else is allowed
    to use that title.
That exclusiveness
indicates
that the king
is the boss.
The others
are his subjects
and they have often
nothing to say at all.
Sometimes those others
are not allowed
to express themselves,

in fact
they are not allowed
to think.
>   When the king passes,
>   all life stops,
>   streets are swept clear,
>   all bow their heads,
>   and sometimes even hold their breaths
>   the king passes
>   them!
Pilate,
being the governor,
was a ruler like that.
Before he arrived
his soldiers
had chased everybody
away from the streets,
officers on horseback
preceded him,
and he himself
did not even look around,
proud as he was:
the others were supposed
to look at him.
>   It was that Pilate,
>   sitting on his throne
>   who asked Jesus,
>   dirty and beaten up already:
>   "Are you king?"
>   and he looked at his soldiers,
>   and the banners,
>   at the flags, the standards,
>   and his bodyguards.
Jesus too
looked at those soldiers,
and the banners,
and the flags, the standards,
and Pilate's bodyguards

and he said:
"Yes,
I am king,
but not like you,
not like you
in the slightest."
>   When you put Jesus' answer
>   in the context of the other
>   scripture readings of today
>   you will find out
>   what he meant.
When Jesus said:
I am king,
he did not say this
as something
that should be applied only
to him.
He said it
in a way
that does not single
himself out
from all the others,
from us.
Listen to the second reading,
in that passage.
Jesus
is called
the faithful witness
who made all of us
a line of kings.
>   Don't you remember
>   how at each baptism
>   this declaration is made:
>   "I am anointing *you*
>   priest, prophet,
>   and KING!"
We are all kings,
we should all be kings,
and act like them.

We are God's masterpiece
of creation,
we are endowed
with our own reason,
with our own feelings,
we are made
in his image.
We should respect ourselves
as such:
our kingship is the reason
that we should never allow ourselves
to be exploited by others.
The kingship of those others
is the reason
that they should never be
exploited by us.
　　　　We very rarely accept
　　　　our kingship.
　　　　We were too often taught
　　　　to accept ourselves
　　　　as failures,
　　　　and that is why others
　　　　can so easily play with us,
　　　　intimidate us,
　　　　and exploit us.
We say of ourselves
after having done something
stupid,
after having sinned,
after having made a mistake:
　　　　"We are only
　　　　human beings . . .
　　　　To err is
　　　　human . . . ",
　　　　and things like
　　　　that.
We don't feel *royal*,
we don't feel *kingly*,
we don't feel *queenly*.

Nevertheless
that is who we are,
like he was,
    and is,
    and will be.
From this point of view
we can learn
from others;
we can learn
from the old and new
African traditions.
     Do you remember
     that student in front of court
     some weeks ago,
     accused of having written down
     his thoughts about
     the situation?
     Do you remember
     how he told his judge:
     "Who are you
     to tell me
     that I should not think?
     Who are you,
     to forbid me
     to analyze the situation
     in which I live?"
Quite some time ago
I was in a meeting
in Masai country.
A government official
was addressing them,
and he spoke,
and he spoke,
for half an hour,
for one hour,
for two hours,
for . . .
     and an old man stood up,
     an old Masai,
     and he said:

"Can't you stop talking,
you have been talking all the time,
do you think
that we can not talk?
Now I am going
to talk
to you."
But some policemen
came to remove him
from the crowd.
    When we are celebrating
    today
    Jesus King,
    we are celebrating
    a king
    who made us
    participate
    in his kingship.
    We are kings too,
    together with him;
    in him
    we are of kingly stock,
    a ROYAL people;
    let us behave like
    that.
And that is why
I would like to suggest
that we,
at the moment of success,
when others come to compliment
and congratulate us,
say:
    "No wonder
    after all:
    I am a human being,
    you know!"
Glory,
glory,
alleluia,
Amen.

INDEX OF SCRIPTURAL TEXTS

296   INDEX OF SCRIPTURAL TEXTS